Praise for *LGBTQ+ Youth*

"Dr. Lee-Anne Gray has created a precious resource — for LGBTQ+ youth; their caregivers, and the people who love them. Written with equal measures scientific rigor and overarching human compassion, this book will inspire hope, raise spirits, and save lives. An essential tool for helping LGBTQ+ youth to flourish, thrive, and triumph."

-**Jennifer Finney Boylan**, Author of
She's Not There: A Life in Two Genders and Long Black Veil

"Lee-Anne Gray's new book, *LGBTQ+ Youth*, is an indispensable guide for assisting our young patients in coming-to-terms with their sexuality, their gender, or both. Seen through an ecological systems perspective, it provides opportunities for adolescents to more fully understand themselves, and promotes ways that we, as clinicians, can facilitate their growth as well as our own. Underneath the practicality of Dr. Gray's approach clearly lies a deep humanity that shines through on every page, exuding not only an appreciation for difference, but a full embrace of it."

-**Andrew R. Gottlieb**, PhD,
Author of *Out of the Twilight: Fathers of Gay Men Speak and Sons Talk About Their Gay Fathers: Life Curves*

"This book is a wonderful resource for youth who are exploring diverse sexual and gender identities. The normalizing and validating language communicates that "who you are is ok!" It is also very comprehensive, discussing a lot of complex ideas and terms in language that is accessible and relatable. For this reason, this book may also be very helpful for parents and clinicians who are working to support LGBT+ youth. The hands-on exercises are designed to help youth foster positive feelings about who they are and to help them to make decisions that are most congruent for them in their journey. LGBT+ youth often feel isolated and utilizing this book lets them know that they are not alone!"

-**Deb Coolhart**, PhD, LMFT,
Co-author of *The Gender Quest Workbook*

"Get a copy for your pediatrician, therapist, GSA, & school counselor today! As a queer-identified transman, parent, and career educator, I recommend Dr. Gray's workbook to every professional who works with LGBTQ+ youth. Parents and caregivers can also learn much about the needs and challenges of their LGBTQ+ children, especially as they navigate extended family, schools, therapists, and medical practitioners. We must educate ourselves and those in charge of our youth when we are not around if we are to change the self-harm, addiction, and school-to-pipeline statistics that plague our LGBTQ+ youth."

-**Christian James Zsilavetz**, MEd.,
Co-founder Pride School Atlanta (Openly affirming school for youth of all ages!)

LGBTQ+ YOUTH

A Guided Workbook to Support Sexual Orientation and Gender Identity

Lee-Anne Gray, PsyD

LGBTQ+ Youth © 2018 by Lee-Anne Gray

Published by
PESI Publishing & Media
PESI, Inc
3839 White Ave
Eau Claire, WI 54703

Editing: Michelle Nelson
Layout: Bookmasters & Amy Rubenzer
Cover: Amy Rubenzer

ISBN: 9781683731382

All rights reserved.

Proudly printed in the United States

About the Author

Lee-Anne Gray, PsyD, is a psychologist, educator, and author. She is certified in EMDR, a trauma treatment, as well as a national speaker in self-compassion, mindful awareness, LGBTQ+ youth, gender, sexuality, assessment, special education, and gifted individuals. She is the president and CEO of The Connect Group, offering innovative professional development seminars in empathy, compassion cultivation, Design Thinking, and self-compassion. Dr. Gray is formerly an instructor of Psychology of Gender in the Departments of Psychology/Women's Studies at UCLA, and has served the LGBTQ+ community as an ally and through her private practice. She was a forensic expert for the Public Defender of Orange County when LGBTQ+ psychological evaluations were needed. Prior to this, Dr. Gray was the supervising psychologist at the largest special education nonprofit organization in the nation.

In 2012, she curated and organized TEDxStudioCityED with the theme of Blending Self-Regulation, Technology, and Education. She is also a contributing author to *Pedagogies of Kindness and Respect: On the Lives and Education of Children (Peter Lang, 2015)* in which she discusses *Educational Trauma* and *Empathic Education for a Compassionate Nation (EECN.)* Along with young people as equal participants, Dr. Gray co-designed EECN to promote co-learning and mitigate *Educational Trauma*. She is the author of *Self-Compassion for Teens: 129 Activities & Practices* and *Self-Compassion and Mindfulness for Teens Card Deck*.

Dedication

This book is dedicated to
LGBTQ+ youth everywhere,
with love and appreciation for your authenticity.

Table Of Contents

Acknowledgments...xi

Introduction...xiii

Part I: Clinician and Educator Toolbox

Chapter

1. Lesbian, Gay, Bisexual & Queer Identity Developement & Coming Out..............................1
2. Lesbian Youth...27
3. Gay Youth...39
4. Bisexual Youth..47
5. Transgender...53
6. Gender Transition..65
7. Questioning Youth...77

Part II: Clinical Approaches to LGBTQ+ Youth Treatment

Chapter

8. Compassion, Countertransference, and Counteraction to LGBTQ+ Youth....................101
9. Training LGBTQ+ Youth in Self-Compassion..119
10. Safety Issues Acceptance and Outcomes..131
11. Making School Safe for LGBTQ+ Youth..145

Appendix A LGBTQ+ Youth Resource List..159

Appendix B Parent Education and Collaboration Handout Pages..161

Appendix C Loving Kindness Practice (Metta)...167

Appendix D Substance Use Self-Test..169

Appendix E Talking about Gender...171

Appendix F Gender Support Plan & Genter Transition Plan..175

References...185

Acknowledgments

First, I'd like to acknowledge the many people who've come before me and whose work I've relied upon to learn and grow as a person, psychologist, educator, and author. They are too numerous to mention though everyone is remembered in this moment. There are many LGBTQ+ people who have been my teachers, and I am grateful to you all! To Jazz Jennings, Jaden Smith, EJ Johnson, Ruby Rose, Miley Cyrus, Lady Gaga, Ellen DeGeneres, Laverne Cox, Hari Nef, Manny Guttierrez, Michael Sam, Janet Mock, Glennon Doyle Melton, Feminista Jones, Jennifer Finney Boylan, Judith Butler, Kimberle Williams Crenshaw, Susan Faludi, and Howard Liebman—you're all very important teachers to me, and your influence can be found in every aspect of this book.

My work with PESI and PESI Publishing & Media continues to be a journey of joy and delight. I am extremely grateful to many people at PESI and PESI Publishing & Media for the opportunities extended my way. Thank you to Meg Mickelson Graf for being my first business manager and for connecting me with Emily Krumenauer to serve PESI's LGBTQ Kids and Teens Seminars. Many thank yous to Emily for co-creating the LGBTQ Seminar with me, upon which this book is based.

In creating books and products for PESI Publishing & Media, I derive great joy and personal enrichment collaborating with Karsyn Morse. She is really like my "first true love" of editors, and continues to hold a special place in my heart. Karsyn, thank you for your guidance, and for the beautiful way you turn ideas into valuable products! And thank you to Linda Jackson for your role in publishing my products, especially this book. Special thanks to Amy Rubenzer for creating a delightful cover and layout to this book. And to Michelle Nelson for catching my typos!

A special and heartfelt thank you is offered to Honor Chervin. Your love and brilliance have inspired me and every aspect of this book, in more ways than you can ever know. Thank you to Jennifer Fraser, PhD, another very brilliant woman who has lovingly contributed to this book and to my personal and professional development: Jen, you're one of the wisest and smartest women I know and I cherish you so! Thank you!

My gratitude for my family and friends is also underscored here. I could not deliver books, products, retreats, programming, seminars, and more without the love, support, and generosity of a few very special people. These people include my special women friends: Wendy Taira and Dena Lazar. Thank you both for doing life with me; it's definitely a better trip with you along!

My family rocks beyond belief—to my kids: Lewis, Chase, and Zoe, thank you for being my co-learners on this adventure of a lifetime! I love you, love learning with you, and love spreading the good word with you, too! To Richard, thank you for the opportunity to love you and be loved by you—this is the greatest gift I've received in this lifetime; it embellishes the love I share and experience everywhere else.

Finally, I'd like to acknowledge all the people who may be touched by this book. Whether you are a professional reading it or the anonymous LGBTQ+ youth who benefits from the adult reading this book, I want you to know I am most thankful for you! Your presence in this world is my gift, and I love you!

Introduction

Welcome!

This book is divided into two parts: The first part is *for clinicians/educators to use with youth*, and includes informative and engaging mindful awareness practices, guided meditations, exercises, and opportunities for LGBTQ+ youth to self-reflect with meaningful handout pages. **The second part focuses on *Individual, Family, & Community Level interventions for the clinician and/or educator***, from an ecological systems perspective. Specific tools, activities, forms, and practices are included for professionals to use in treatment and lesson planning, school care, family counseling, and community advocacy. Self-reflective activities for the professional are also included, in this part, to reduce countertransference, counterreaction, implicit bias, and stereotyping.

Chapter One begins with lesbian, gay, bisexual and questioning identification development, as well as coming out.

LGB&Q+ identity development is introduced with definitions and terminology, then explored by building on the work of Kinsey, and later Klein. (**Transgender and intersex identity development will be addressed separately, because the evolution of gender differs from sexual orientation identity development.**) Internalized homo/bi–phobia are obstacles youth must overcome to integrate their authentic identity in a healthy way. Moving from one identity to another, from cultural acceptance to cultural threat, complicates the identity journey teens already go through in reaching adulthood. However, it need not be painful, and can be quite joyful!

The exercises and worksheets in Chapter One focus on: terms & definitions, sexual orientation identity formation, and the complexity of sexuality. The decision to come out can involve safety risks. Safety planning is also included in the worksheets provided so LGBTQ+ youth can plan and create coming out strategies that promote their health and well-being. The chapter closes out with how LGB&Q+ youth can talk with others about their identity.

In Chapter Two, on Lesbian Youth, issues like invisibility, increased need to facilitate positive self-regard and self-worth, as well as sexual health and development are presented. Homophobia, misogyny, and transmisogyny originate in society, but can infect the internal experience of lesbian youth. For these reasons, the chapter directly addresses the negative impact of these attitudes. Dating and wanting and initiating sex are also themes that arise for some lesbian youth. Assisting them in managing these and related issues, like sleepovers, sex, and parents are also included in Chapter Two. Drug and alcohol use is quite high in the LGBTQ+ youth community, and especially so among lesbian youth. As such, this issue is addressed with a self-test youth can take to explore the nature of their substance use. Finally, lesbian youth in sports represent a unique population and are addressed here in an effort to mitigate the challenges faced in competitive sports.

Chapter Three, on Gay Youth, discusses male gender role expectations, and how being gay expands beyond norms, among other issues, too. Research shows that gay identity development in adolescence is correlated with intimacy, relationship fulfillment, and intimate partner violence

(Edwards & Sylaska, 2012.) Sexual health and the impact of the HIV crisis endures in gay communities, and therefore deserves some elucidation as young gay men develop. With substance use also a concern in the gay community, it is explored with a self-test youth can take to assess their use. Body image is also addressed, as it is a clinical concern for some gay youth.

Understanding bisexuality as a legitimate and distinct identity remains a crucial concern that impacts youth who love males, females, and more. **Chapter Four, on Bisexual Youth,** explores the nuances and struggles of youth loving diverse humans. The harmfulness of bisexual erasure is addressed, along with a self-test (in Appendix D) for substance abuse owing to the very high risk of addiction in bisexual youth (Marshal et al, 2008).

The focus shifts away from sexual orientation to gender identity in **Chapter Five, on Transgender and Intersex Identity Development.** Exploring options for gender expression, gender expansiveness, and gender expansive youth are introduced along with definitions of terms. The rainbow of gender identities and expression are elucidated in the Gray Gender Spectrum exploring multiple dimensions of gender identity, as well as how expression varies over time. Since not all who are gender expansive wish to transition, some issues are introduced here and followed up in Chapter Seven on Questioning Youth. The fluidity of gender is explored with details about how to identify and treat gender dysphoria. Differential diagnosis with body dysmorphic disorder is easy when the contrast is highlighted. Moreover, self-love and body confidence can increase with clinician and educator sensitivity. Names and pronouns are a unique clinical theme that emerges for transyouth. Chapter Five shows professionals how to address this key issue. Internalized transphobia can complicate healthy gender identity development and/or transition; therefore, it is explored here with some education presented in interactive worksheets. Finally, the chapter concludes with a brief exploration of intersex identity development and the unique features of identity development that follow this biological condition.

Chapter Six, on Gender Transition, promotes collaboration between clinicians and youth in assessing need/desire for gender transition. It guides transition with influence from the World Professional Association of Transgender Health (WPATH) and the Harry Benjamin Standards of Care (7th Revision) so clinicians can feel comfortable documenting for risk management. Clinicians who worry about authorizing and facilitating transition can use tools from this chapter to collaborate, affirm, empathize, and care for gender expansive youth. Looking at which aspects of transition appeal and which don't helps transyouth discover the kind of transition (if any) that is best for them. New to the literature are the concepts of Developmental Gender and Chronological Gender. These terms capture the unique trajectory of development that transpeople go through if and when they decide to transition. The chapter also shows professionals how to assess the level of distress transyouth feel about their gender. This assessment is critical to affirming transition because it documents how greatly transyouth suffer.

Gender and sexuality can feel rigid and defined, especially in our culture. Questioning youth, addressed in Chapter Seven, remind us that this is an illusion. **Chapter Seven explores fluidity and openness to both gender and sexuality.** It offers youth and professionals an opportunity to explore sexual and gender identity, with openness and without the need to label. For some people, this is a stage they pass through before realizing they are gay or trans. For other people, being queer is the state of being. It can also be a period of exploration for youth who may ultimately decide to transition. Whichever need it serves, let it be a time of celebration, curiosity, and love.

Part II of this book changes in focus and audience, as it is intended primarily for the professional who works with LGBTQ+ youth in clinical and educational settings. The second part focuses on strategies and approaches to LGBTQ+ youth, from an ecological systems perspective.

Bronfenbrenner's (1979) ecological systems theory suggests that people are part of an interconnected, yet related, system with the individual at the center. LGBTQ+ youth, for example, are inseparable unique elements of a social network, and are simultaneously impacted by the social network. When empathizing with LGBTQ+ youth through the lens of Bronfenbrenner's ecological-systems theory, they are understood in terms of the impact surrounding systems have upon them. This is the framework used for Part II, and also for understanding Educational Trauma, which severely impacts LGBTQ+ youth.

The first chapter in Part II is one of two that address the individual level of ecological systems. It focuses the professional's attention to their reactions and biases in order to deepen the level of compassion offered to LGBTQ+ youth. It demonstrates how to apply compassion strategies and interventions (Paul Gilbert) to LGBTQ+ youth, as well as how to manage the countertransference/counterreactions that interfere with compassion and treatment. LGBTQ+ youth can present with very strong transference reactions. This phenomenon is explained for clinicians and educators, along with tips for how to respond in a favorable and helpful manner. This chapter also applies Acceptance and Commitment Therapy (ACT) principles to LGBTQ+ youth and their unique concerns, and concludes with Paul Gilbert's (2009) compassion circles.

Chapter Nine shows professionals how to introduce self-compassion practices to LGBTQ+ youth. Self-compassion is associated with decreased depression and anxiety, as well as increased well-being. When applied to LGBTQ+ youth, the power arises in mitigating the effects of the extreme discrimination they face. Because of the role and prevalence of trauma in the lives of LGBTQ+ youth, they experience disproportionately high self-loathing, rejection, abuse, abandonment, homelessness, and suicidality. Reducing the risk of dissociation and decompensation due to increased rates of traumatization is an important clinical responsibility when treating LGBTQ+ youth. Self-compassion strategies for LGBTQ+ youth are offered in the Self-Compassion Training Protocol for Traumatized Teens (Gray, 2016), adapted for LGBTQ+ youth, to promote healthy forms of courage, vulnerability, bravery, and self-kindness. Trauma effects can be mitigated with interventions that promote acceptance, commitment, and the willingness to take action to relieve suffering. However, professionals need cognitive and psychological flexibility, which are key aspects of Acceptance and Commitment Therapy (ACT), to do so. The key aspects of ACT are adapted into worksheets for clinicians to use in self-managing countertransference, counterreaction, unintended bias, and LGBTQ+ youth transference, too.

Chapter Ten takes a look at how to collaborate with families of LGBTQ+ youth. It includes offering safety for parental reactions of grief, loss, disappointment, resistance, fear, aversion, worry, and sparing youth from these reactions. Interventions are offered to help clinicians assess and explore the family's readiness to support LGBTQ+ youth. The importance of parental support in long-term outcomes for LGBTQ+ youth influences this chapter. Religion is also explored as it can be a strong confounding variable in the development of LGBTQ+ youth.

To conclude this workbook, **Chapter Eleven looks at the community level and how to make schools safe for LGBTQ+ youth.** This angle rounds out Part II, by offering strategies for creating GSAs and Safe Zones in schools, where LGBTQ+ youth know they can speak freely. Social justice in schools is an ethical responsibility for school counselors. This chapter shows professionals how to meet this ethical standard with a checklist and a shortened questionnaire to assist efforts. Form letters are included to inspire professionals to act on behalf of LGBTQ+ youth bullied, mistreated, and/or having bathroom/locker room issues. Knowing how to speak with and train youth and other professionals in being kind to LGBTQ+ youth is critical to making schools safe, which is why this is a focal point of Chapter Eleven. Finally, it covers the heinous effects of the school-to-prison pipeline, and the steps professionals can take to do their part in dismantling it.

There are six appendices included in this workbook. The first one contains resources that may be important to LGBTQ+ youth and the adults in their lives. Appendix B holds handouts for parents, including activities and facts/stats/data sheets. Appendix C is instructions for the Loving Kindness practice, which supports several elements of cultivating self-compassion. Appendix D is a substance abuse self-test developed for LGBTQ+ youth to self-assess their use of drugs and alcohol. It is followed by Appendix E which includes forms from Gender Spectrum to guide professionals in supporting students who are transitioning and/or gender expansive. Appendix F includes possible statements and responses to common questions parents and others have about teaching gender, supporting gender-creative students, and facilitating inclusive affirming.

> Worksheets and exercises that are boxed in are meant to be reproduced and given directly to youth.

PART I
Clinician and Educator Toolbox

Introduction to Part I

Welcome to Part I of this guided workbook! Use the various elements for a wide range of ages, according to your professional discretion. Beginning with Chapter One, there are interactive sheets you can use with youth to explore sexual orientation identity development; coming out & safety planning.

In Chapter Two, the focus shifts exclusively to the needs and issues germane to lesbian youth. Sex, dating, sleepovers, parents, and even substance abuse are addressed in Chapter Two.

Moving along to gay youth, Chapter Three explores gender roles and expectations as they intersect with sexuality in males; sexual health, and body image.

Commonly erased and unseen our bisexual youth are calling for inclusion and Chapter Four facilities just that!

Chapters Five and Six focus on gender identity development, particularly for transgender and intersex youth. Find activities to use with youth to help them explore their identity and relationship to self and others. There are also templates and form letters to assist in advocating for bathroom/locker room use, as well as for affirming readiness to transition.

Part I concludes with Chapter Seven on questioning youth who have the distinct right and invitation to be fluid and explore gender and/or sexuality without the pressure to label

Lesbian, Gay Bisexual & Queer Identity Development & Coming Out

---

Lesbian, gay, bisexual, and some queer identities develop in similar ways. In this chapter, we will explore the process of realizing you're gay, lesbian, bisexual, or something else. We will look at the different identities and terminologies, because there are a lot more than just gay, lesbian, and bisexual. By examining the stages of identity formation you may go through, and how to talk with others about it, too. Internalized homo/bi–phobia are obstacles you may encounter, and need to overcome in order to synthesize authentic identity in a healthy way.

Coming out is an element of being lesbian, gay, and bisexual. Not everyone decides to come out, nor does so in the same way or time. This process of sharing your authentic nature with others will also be explored in this chapter. For some, it can be truly affirming and for others it can involve threat to safety. Both possibilities, and more, are explored in this chapter.

1. GROUNDING AND CENTERING MEDITATION FOR IDENTITY DEVELOPMENT

LEARN

The joy of becoming you is amplified when your sense of Self is well-defined. Growing up can involve a tug of war that goes on inside and/or with others—particularly parents. The following guided meditation helps with the self-defining process by anchoring you in the present moment. You can record yourself saying it or have your trusted adult do it for you. Listening to this meditation creates the internal conditions and brain wiring for the healthy development of your Self. This sort of thing is basic for all people, and really important to affirming LGBQ+ identities and coming out with ease and grace.

PRACTICE

- Find a comfortable position, seated, standing, or even lying down.

- Notice your body and where it makes contact with the ground and/or the furniture.

- Close your eyes, if you feel comfortable.

- Take three deep breaths all the way down into your belly.

- Feel the air inflating your chest as it enters your body through your nose.

- Notice the sensations in your belly as you breathe deeply.

- Now imagine there is a connector at the base of your tailbone.

- Examine the width and color of this connector, then attach a cord to it.

- The cord can be any color, width, or thickness; there is no right or wrong here.

- See the cord drop down through the floor beneath you, magically and instantly penetrating the crust of the Earth and connecting to the core.

- When your grounding cord is connected to the Earth's core, you are "grounded" and "centered." People often report feeling energized, and radically alive.

- Now that you are grounded, notice a yellow sun hovering around your forehead where it meets the bridge of your nose.

- Invite this special yellow sun to collect all of your energy that may have been scattered about as you made your way through the day. Silently say to yourself:

> *Yellow sun of mine, please collect any and all of my energy that may have been scattered about. Please purify it, recharge it, and return it to me.*

- When you are ready, allow your cleansed energy to shower down upon you like a raindrop of yellow light.

- See the yellow light envelope you, and fill the space around you within the drop.

- Enjoy this special space for as long as you like.

- When you are ready, take a deep breath, and open your eyes.

REFLECT

- If you use this meditation every day, it helps promote healthy interdependence through grounding and centering.

- Grounding and centering are terms that relate to being well-regulated, balanced, and radically alive.

- Explore any reasons why you may/may not wish to practice this meditation.

2. TERMS AND IDENTITIES

LEARN

There are many more sexual and gender identities than gay/straight; male/female; trans/cis. If any of these terms seem new to you, let's explore them. If they aren't new to you, then remember this page the next time you encounter someone who may not know about them.

One important distinction:

Sex: Determined based on biological markers, such as genitals and chromosomes (XX = female; XY = male, etc.)

Sexuality: Whom you are sexually attracted to

Gender: Who *you* are, as determined by *you*, not your genitals or chromosomes

PRACTICE

Define and discuss the following terms:

SEXUALITY:

Lesbian _____

Gay _____

Bisexual _____

Queer _____

Questioning _____

Homosexual _____

Same-gender loving _____

Ally _____

Pansexual _____

Straight _____

Heterosexual _____

Skoliosexual _____

Omnisexual _____

Polysexual _____

Polyamory _____

Grey Ace _____

Asexual _____

GENDER:

Pangender _____

Cisgender _____

Transgender _____

Intersex _____

Third Gender _____

Fa'afafine _____

AFAB _____

AMAB _____

Non-binary _____

Gender expansive _____

Gender fluid _____

Genderqueer _____

Agender _____

Demiboy _____

Demigirl _____

Androgyne _____

Intergender _____

REFLECT: Read over answer key.

Sexuality:

- Lesbian – refers to females who are sexually attracted to other females. This includes transfemales who love other females and transfemales.

- Gay – refers to males who are sexually attracted to males, as well as transmales who love men and other transmen.

- Bisexual – sexual desire for, and attraction to, both males and females (may or may not include transmales and transfemales).

- Queer – is an umbrella term members of the LGBTQ+ community may or may not identify with. It is self-applied, and used to be a pejorative term, now claimed by the LGBTQ+ community as an empowered term. It is important to use caution with this term. Like other terms re-appropriated by marginalized communities, it is not favored when used by members outside the community.

- Questioning – is an umbrella term for people who are figuring themselves out, discovering the rainbow of human sexuality and/or gender, and still in the process of finding their place.

- Homosexual – is a general term for people who are sexually attracted to others of the same gender, and can include gay, lesbian, bisexual, and transpeople.

- Same-gender loving – is a gender expansive and inclusive term for those who love others of the same gender. It can include gender expansive people who don't fit the binary (gay/straight/bi).

- Ally – anyone willing to stand up for the freedom to love and be loved!

- Pansexual – (also Omnisexual) is sexual attraction to people regardless of their sex or gender identity.

- Straight – is another term for being sexually attracted to males if you're female, and females if you're male.

- Heterosexual – is another term for being straight.

- Skoliosexual – sexual attraction to non-binary people.

- Grey Ace – sometimes asexual, sometimes not.

- Polysexual – being attracted to people of more than one gender, but not all genders.

- Polyamory – having multiple romantic, emotional, and sexual relationships without the expectation of monogamy.

- Asexual – no interest in sexual activity.

Gender:

- Pangender – a person who identifies with all genders, especially inclusive of the non-binary gender identities that go beyond male and female.

- Cisgender – when one's gender identity matches the gender assigned at birth.

- Transgender – when one's assigned gender at birth doesn't match their internal psychological experience of gender.

- Third Gender – a category that exists in some cultures where the individual or society determines they are neither male nor female.

- Fa'afafine – Samoans who identify as Third Gender.

- Intersex – when an infant is born with ambiguous genitalia, efforts to assign gender at birth become complicated. Intersex individuals represent the biological intersection of sex and gender.

- AFAB – acronym for Assigned Female at Birth.

- AMAB – acronym for Assigned Male at Birth.

- Non-binary – gender non-conforming or expansive people.

- Gender expansive – people for whom the gender binary of male and female just don't apply.

- Gender fluid – people who experience their gender in fluid, changing, and variable ways.

- Demiboy – partly a boy, partly something else not defined.

- Demigirl – partly a girl, partly something else not defined.

- Androgyne – having both masculine and feminine characteristics; embodying and appearing to be both male and female at once. Pertaining to androgyny and/or gender ambiguity.

- Agender – people for whom no gender applies.

- Intergender – Another term for intersex; also gender identity that is among or in the midst of the gender binary of male/masculine and female/feminine.

3. GRAY'S SEXUAL ORIENTATION GRID

LEARN

Alfred Kinsey (1948) was the first to tip us off to the range of human sexual expression. Kinsey developed a rating scale used in research to determine a person's homo-eroticism and hetero-eroticism—their level of sexual attraction to people of the same or another gender. He helped us first see that males could be sexually attracted to other males, females, both at the same time, and even at different times. Later, he showed the same for females and how fluid their sexual attraction could be. Fritz Klein (1993) came around later on and introduced some more complexity to this party. He presented sexuality in a grid he called the Klein Sexual Orientation Grid. The contributions of these two pioneers in sex research are synthesized in the practice below, and updated to be non-binary in nature.

Using the rating scale below, explore for yourself where you land. You don't have to share it with anyone else, but it's here so you can see how many variations of love, sex, and attraction are healthy and ok! The gray area of sexuality between heterosexuality and homosexuality is very diverse and quite colorful too!

PRACTICE: Fill out the following grid.

REFLECT

- Remembering the work of Kinsey, and Klein afterwards, helps us see how science is crawling along to understand the diversity of human love, sex, and gender.

- Millennials may already know people are hardwired for gender and sexual fluidity, while parents and grandparents may still be stuck in the binaries of the past.

- After you know where you stand on the grid, remember it can and may change, or it may not. You can refer older people to Kinsey's and Klein's work if they need to self-educate.

- Willful ignorance is dangerous, yet prevalent. You can do your part by knowing the scientists' names behind sex research.

How do you self-label?

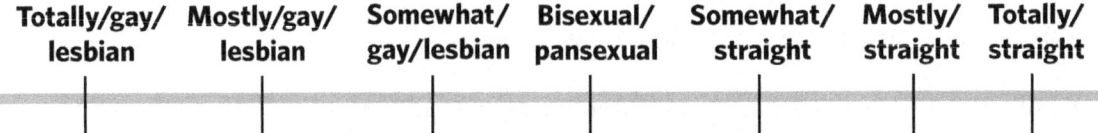

*Other: Please identify the gender you are most attracted to, if one stands out. If not, there's no need to identify. Additionally, you can always keep it private, until you're ready to share.

Copyright © 2018 Lee-Anne Gray. *LGBTQ+ Youth*. All rights reserved.

GRAY'S SEXUAL ORIENTATION GRID

	My gender only	My gender mostly	My gender somewhat more	All genders equally	*Other gender somewhat more	*Other gender mostly	*Other gender only	Past	Present	Ideal
Who are you attracted to?										
Who do you actually have sex with?										
Whom do you fantasize about having sex with?										
Who do you have a personal preference for hanging out with?										
With whom do you have a special emotional connection?										
Which community do you prefer to hang out with?										

(Inspired by Klein, 1993)

Copyright © 2018 Lee-Anne Gray. *LGBTQ+ Youth*. All rights reserved.

4. MULTI-DIMENSIONAL SEXUAL IDENTITY FORMATION

LEARN

If you've just completed Gray's Sexual Orientation Grid, you're so far ahead of the game! For others who may still be on the path to figuring out some of this stuff, here's a multi-dimensional look at what some people go through in discovering they're LG&B+. Take a look and see where you land on the path of self-discovery.

PRACTICE

Multi-Dimensional Sexual Identity Formation:

Inside Dimensions:	Outside Dimensions:
Confusion	Pride
Comparison	Synthesizing it all
Tolerating oneself	Disclosing identity to friends
Accepting oneself and differences	Disclosing to members of the immediate family
Feeling different	Disclosing to members of the extended family
Self-labeling	Disclosing to people at school or work
Coming in to authentic identity	

(Adapted from Coolhart, 2016; Cass, 1979; Stone Fish & Harvey, 2005; Savin-Williams, 1990)

REFLECT

- Although the Inside and Outside Dimensions of identity formation are presented in lists that make it look like one feature evolves into the next, it doesn't necessarily work like that. People can bounce around between internal and external identity formation dimensions in a non-linear way.

- Sexuality, gender, and the development of Self arise in unique ways for everyone. Even if similarities exist between people, there are still many variations.

- Use the internal and external dimensions of LG&B+ identity formation to see where you are on your path. Doing so is an act of self-empathy (Gray, 2016).

5. FEARS ABOUT COMING OUT

LEARN

Despite some protections and inclusion of LGBTQ+ individuals, the truth is it's still dangerous out there for many. In the following activity page, explore the fears you have about coming out. They may be reality-based, or not; it doesn't matter. This is a time and place to release fears of all kinds.

PRACTICE

On the lines provided below, list all the fears, worries, insecurities, and possible negative outcomes that could arise when/if you come out:

_____
_____
_____
_____
_____
_____
_____
_____
_____
_____
_____
_____

Now, circle the top three most likely to occur, and cross out the three that are least likely to occur.

REFLECT

- Some fears are reality-based and some are creations of our mind. It takes time and attention to figure out the difference. By listing all your fears, you can begin to familiarize yourself with them and then see which were worth paying attention to and which ones were not.

- If you have any fears about your safety, please complete the Safety Planning activity on page 14, too. It helps you figure out back-up plans, if things get really messed up.

6. FEARS ABOUT COMING OUT II

LEARN

The process of you affirming your LGBTQ+ identity can be one that also arouses fear and worry. This is common, though sadly it can lead to depression, anxiety, social isolation, more worry, and thoughts of harming/killing oneself. In the section, answer the questions, and reflect on any fears you may have about coming out. For some of you, there may be many fears; for others, not so many. It's ok; there's no right or wrong reaction here. (If you even think about harming/killing yourself, please turn to the adult who gave this sheet to you, or the Trevor Project. Helpful resources, including a link to the Trevor Project's website, are located in Appendix A.)

PRACTICE

How did you react to you the first time you realized you were LGBTQ+?

_____

_____

_____

_____

How do you imagine your parents will react to you, when/if you come out to them?

_____

_____

_____

_____

How do you imagine your family members will react to you, when/if you come out to them?

_____

_____

_____

_____

How do you imagine your friends and acquaintances will react to you, when/if you come out to them?

_____

_____

_____

_____

REFLECT

- Explore the impact and effects of coming out, as you see and imagine it.

- It's ok to think about how others may react; just remember that we have no way of knowing what goes on in other people's minds. It's just a guess, until they confirm or disconfirm the hypotheses.

- After writing down your fears, silently offer them to the universe, releasing that which no longer serves you. You can say something like this:

> *I choose to release fears and feelings that do not serve my highest good.*

- Find an adult you feel comfortable talking about this with, and discover some of the positive things that could emerge when you release ideas that do not serve you.

7. SAFETY PLANNING

LEARN

Coming out should be a time of affirmation and authenticity, but can be a time of danger. LGBTQ+ youth can be rejected, assaulted, and harmed for expressing their identity and loving others. Safety planning is really important when some LGBTQ+ youth think about coming out. Some don't have these concerns, but because so many do, it's really important to ask yourself if you see any risks in coming out. If you do, please know you are not alone. There are resources (in Appendix A) at the end of this book where you can find even more support, if needed.

PRACTICE

Are there any risks that you can think of happening, if you tell your parents you are LGBTQ+?

_____
_____
_____
_____

If any of these things happen, whom can you turn to for help? List all of them here, even if they are a maybe.

_____
_____
_____
_____

When you are afraid, what do you do to care for yourself?

_____
_____
_____
_____

Brainstorm all the ways you can strengthen your courage and bravery muscles:

_____

_____

_____

REFLECT

- It's very challenging for some people to come out to their family, even when they may already be out to their friends. This is normal. It's also common for some families to be unsupportive, while others are.

- See if you can find strength for yourself, while also allowing your parents and family to be however they need to be.

- If there are true safety risks to coming out, please make sure you've sought guidance in how to handle it, and have a few back-up plans in case things get rough.

- Explore the list of resources in Appendix A to see if any could be included in the list of people you can call on at any time of day, if you need help.

- Completing this activity page doesn't mean you're in danger if you come out. It means you are preparing for difficult possibilities that are common when people affirm something that is inconsistent with the dominant culture.

- Another benefit to this activity is noticing your perceived risks of coming out, and it gives you the opportunity to examine how realistic those fears are. Some may be really understandable threats, while others could be your mind getting worked up. It's hard to tell the difference, so planning for difficulties gives you a way out until you can tell the difference.

8. DECIDING TO COME OUT

LEARN

How do you know when you're ready to come out to others? How do you know that you have the courage and bravery to be you, even if it means going against the stream? Explore the questions to see if you are ready, or what might be needed for you to feel comfortable and come out.

PRACTICE

How long ago did you notice you felt this way?

_____

_____

_____

When you think about yourself, do you feel like you want to identify out loud as gay, lesbian, and/or bisexual? Why or why not?

_____

_____

_____

When you imagine yourself coming out to another person, how does it play out in your mind?

_____

_____

_____

Does coming out seem like an important step for you to affirm your identity?

_____

_____

_____

What is your opinion of those who decide not to come out?

_____

_____

_____

Can you see your life being fulfilling and rewarding if you never come out, or only come out to some people?

_____

_____

_____

REFLECT

- Coming out is hard for some people, mainly because our culture doesn't truly support it. Gains have surely been made, and then rolled back. These instances, as well as the laws that guide our culture, convey lack of acceptance for people who are different.

- If you have any misgivings or hesitation about coming out, please be kind to yourself. Practice self-compassion by being gentle about your expectations for yourself and for others (Gray, 2016).

- If you feel ready and excited to come out and tell people who you really are, let's celebrate with cartwheels and fireworks!

- Any reaction you have to coming out is ok, and may change over time.

- Be open to changes in your opinion about coming out, and notice how it fluctuates as your identity deepens.

9. COMMUNICATING WITH OTHERS ABOUT LGBT&Q IDENTITY

LEARN

How one conveys a message can have a lot of impact on how it is received. Yeah, it's kind of weird, but how we say things can lead people to ideas and stories that are not even intended at all! When it comes to something as important as who you are, you may wish to express yourself in a way that honors you and the other person. How might you bring clarity, respect, kindness, and empathy to your coming out? For you and for your listener? Good news! Here are some questions you can reflect upon to synthesize some great statements:

PRACTICE

Who are you?

_____
_____
_____
_____

How do you want others to see you?

_____
_____
_____
_____

In the space provided below, write a few different statements you could use to tell people you are LGBTQ+. They don't have to be perfect, just write some stuff down.

_____
_____
_____
_____

Let's bring it all together by reviewing your answers to the first three questions. See if you can blend it all up and come up with something that is really authentic and courageous.

REFLECT

- You don't ever have to say these words out loud or share them with anyone until and unless you are ready; however, completing these few questions helps you get clear about what you might want to say.

- Getting clear about what you want to say stems from knowing who you are and taking the time to find the words to convey it to others.

- For some people, saying they are LGBTQ+ is easy, self-evident, and self-explanatory. For others, not so much…

- Practicing writing/talking about it helps.

10. IS YOUR FAMILY READY FOR YOU TO COME OUT?

LEARN

Research shows that family acceptance has a strong influence on how well LGBTQ+ youth turn out (Ryan, 2009). When young people come out, they've already been on the journey for quite some time. For their parents and family members, the journey is just beginning. I call this phenomenon *Family's Unique Time Zones*. Each member is in their own time zone about coming out. Sometimes, the family members synch up, and sometimes it takes time or doesn't happen at all. The following activity helps you think through some things about your family's readiness. Don't fret if it doesn't look good at first; everything is impermanent—the good and the bad!

PRACTICE

When you think about your family, how open are they to new things?

_____
_____
_____

Are they very religious? Not at all? A little? Traditional?

_____
_____
_____

Do their values match yours?

_____
_____
_____

How do your parents react to stories in the news about LGBTQ+ people? Do they judge? Are they mad about the injustices? Are they critical? Do they live and let others live?

_____
_____
_____

Are your parents inclusive of other people?

___

Have you seen your parents grow and change? Do they fear change/seek growth?

___

REFLECT

- The questions you just explored help you become more mindful about your parents. They may have revealed new things to you, and maybe not. Both are ok.

- The point of exploring these questions is to get a clearer sense of where your parents may be at on the topics of gender expression and sexual orientation.

- In situations where young people come out to their parents, empathy is needed on both sides. This practice helps you become more empathic towards your parents. It's not that they need it more than you, or you more than them, it's just that the more empathy there is to go around, the better it will go for you!

11. DISCHARGING INTERNALIZED HOMOPHOBIA AND BIPHOBIA

LEARN

The world we live in influences us even when we resist and seek to express our authentic selves. The dominant culture infuses us all; the way we relate to it is our choice. When people notice they are attracted to people other than the opposite gender, it can come with internalized homophobia/biphobia, or not. Some internalized homo/biphobia can be noticeable, and often it can be subtle and hardly noticeable.

PRACTICE

Reflect on your emerging sexual identity. What about it makes you proud?

_____
_____
_____

Does anything leave you feeling ashamed?

_____
_____
_____

Is there anything about being gay, lesbian, bisexual, and/or queer that you'd like to hide?

_____
_____
_____

REFLECT

- Reflecting on these questions is one step towards identifying the presence of internalized homophobia.

- It's hard to recognize self-hatred. We all want to deny it straight out, because it isn't any fun at all to feel. On the other hand, it takes great courage, strength, and bravery to look at the dark parts of ourselves. Shining a little light on this issue is one step towards clearing and releasing it.

12. FACING HOMOPHOBIA IN OTHERS

LEARN

The downside of being a part of a minority group is facing the rejection and disapproval of others in the dominant group. Expressing your true and authentic identity may unfortunately bring you face-to-face with discrimination. How you respond to this may influence the outcome for you. You can't control other people, how they treat you and whether or not they bully you. But you can create responses that carve out space for safety and protection.

PRACTICE

Let's say you face an unkind person while you're with someone you love. What are some responses you could offer? Or maybe you would choose not to respond. Why or why not?

___

___

___

___

If you hear from a friend that someone you know said horrible things about you because you are gay, lesbian, bisexual, or queer, it will probably hurt a lot. The pain can make it hard to find words and self-protect. Take the time now to brainstorm some responses. Practice with your trusted adult, and see if they have some helpful tips.

___

___

___

___

Maybe some of your friends have had this happen to them. Ask them what they wish they would've said at the time.

___

___

___

___

REFLECT

- It isn't possible to imagine all the possible unkind comments homophobic people could send your way. Try to realize that no matter how much you prepare for this, it may still come as a surprise if/when it happens.

- The purpose of coming up with a few phrases, even if you can't come up with them all, is to get your brain thinking along these ways.

13. SUBSTANCE ABUSE

LEARN

According to Marshal et al. (2008), LGBTQ+ youth are 190 percent more likely to use drugs or alcohol than heterosexual youth. Bisexual youth are 340% more likely to use substances.

- Not all LGBTQ+ youth use drugs and alcohol. It's ok if this doesn't apply to you; just ignore it.

PRACTICE

Explore your relationship to drugs and alcohol using the Substance Use Self-Test in Appendix D.

REFLECT

- Because drug and alcohol use among LGBTQ+ youth is so high, it's really important to think about this issue.

- Explore it with your friends if you don't think the adults in your life will understand.

Lesbian Youth

This chapter addresses issues confronting lesbian youth including misogyny/transmisogyny, identity and coming out, sex, dating, sleepovers, and parents, as well as substance abuse, sexual health, and development. Lesbian youth in sports represent a unique population that will be addressed here in an effort to mitigate the challenges faced in competitive sports.

1. BULLYING, HOMOPHOBIA, MISOGYNY, AND TRANSMISOGYNY

LEARN

Lesbian youth face different kinds of harassment from gay, bisexual, and transyouth, with some overlap. Distinguishing the unique experiences of lesbian youth requires sensitivity and empathy, as well as careful listening to individual stories. The following checklist is intended for lesbian youth to identify the various forms of discrimination and harassment. Be alert to the micro-aggressions which resemble those of women and other minorities, but are likely amplified because of intersectional influences (race, ethnicity, religion, disability, socioeconomic status, etc.). Moreover, lesbian youth need assistance increasing their ability to identify micro-aggressions, which are subtle, easily overlooked, and often excused.

PRACTICE I

Check off all the situations you've seen or experienced. It doesn't matter if it happened to you or someone else; knowing about it or seeing it happen is also really rough.

- ☐ I've been called a dyke to my face.
- ☐ I've been called a dyke behind my back.
- ☐ I've been called a lipstick/femme lesbian to my face.
- ☐ I've been called a lipstick/femme lesbian behind my back.
- ☐ I've been called butch to my face.
- ☐ I've been called butch behind my back.
- ☐ I've been underestimated, dismissed, and/or passed over for an award, position, or role.
- ☐ I've been punished at school for holding hands with my girlfriend.
- ☐ I've been bullied by other students because I have a girlfriend.
- ☐ Religious people say I'll go to hell.
- ☐ Others get confused about me liking girls, and think I want to be a guy.
- ☐ Being trans and a lesbian at the same time has brought double trouble—other students make fun of me and threaten me.
- ☐ Bisexual students make the most fun of me.
- ☐ I sometimes hate that I am attracted to other girls because it comes with bullying and harassment.
- ☐ _____
  (Fill in the blank if there are others not listed previously.)

PRACTICE II

Explore the following terms, and see if you can recall any experiences that sound this way.

Homophobia: Discrimination and oppression due to sexual orientation. List experiences of homophobia you've experienced, witnessed, or heard about.

_____

_____

_____

Misogyny: Discrimination and oppression originating in hatred, resentment, and jealousy of women. List experiences of misogyny you've experienced, witnessed, or heard about.

_____

_____

_____

Transmisogyny: Discrimination and oppression of transwomen due to gender identity and/or sexual orientation. Although gender and sexuality are not linked, transwomen face enormous violence around their sexuality. List experiences of transmisogyny you've experienced, witnessed, or heard about.

_____

_____

_____

REFLECT

- The experiences listed above are only a short list… Lesbian youth experience many different kinds of bullying—talk about it.

- Even if the adults in your life don't know what it's like for you to be a lesbian in your school/community, you can tell them and they may learn.

- If some of the harassment is coming from staff at your school or youth organization, find an adult whom you can trust. Easier said than done? Ok, keep looking.

- Persistence, tenacity, and the willingness to take action to relive suffering are aspects of self-compassion, which reduce the negative effects of bullying. Practice self-compassion.

2. IDENTITY EXPRESSION AND COMING OUT

LEARN

Lesbian youth express their identity in very diverse and wide ranging ways.

PRACTICE

Describe and explore the ways you express your identity, or keep it private.

_____

_____

_____

Explore how you feel about coming out. Is it comfortable to share with friends, family, strangers, and acquaintances?

_____

_____

_____

REFLECT

- It's ok to feel more comfortable coming out with some people, and less comfortable with others.

- Avoid self-judgment about where you are in the coming out process.

3. DATING

LEARN

Lesbian youth have some role models for dating, romance, and sex. At the same time, power dynamics tend to be re-created within their relationships; some looking like dominance and submission, while others lean towards creating their own rituals. It's important to know that the way lesbian youth and their partners relate need not conform to any pre-existing models, and that power differentials exist in a wide range of relationships.

PRACTICE

Offer lesbian youth a chance to discuss topics of dating, romance, and sex. Invite them to be creative and invent ways of relating that work for them.

REFLECT

If this is new to you, the adult caregiver, let your lesbian youth be your expert. It's ok to switch roles sometimes and learn from young people. In doing so, it also conveys that it's ok to create patterns of relating that work for them, even if they are different.

4. INITIATING SEX

LEARN

Cultural stereotypes can contribute to challenges lesbian youth experience initiating sex. This isn't an issue for all lesbian youth, but can be a problem for some. With females socialized to be more passive in intimate relations, it can be a challenge for lesbian youth to enjoy sexual relations.

PRACTICE

- This practice is a gentle reminder about talking with youth about sex, particularly lesbian youth.

- Don't hesitate to tell lesbian youth it's ok to talk with you about sex.

- Be direct and unafraid to address sexuality and diverse ways of loving people.

- Help them see there are many different ways of relating sexually, and talking about it with their partner is how they can figure out what works for them.

- Invite lesbian youth to tell you their romantic stories and/or experiences, only if they feel comfortable.

- By letting lesbian youth know you are comfortable discussing this topic, you let them know you have empathy for their unique situation and challenges.

- It's ok if this practice never gets further than the invitation to talk.

- Letting lesbian youth know you're there for them around difficult topics is a gift!

REFLECT

- Exploring sex requires courage, self-containment, and great empathy—on the part of youth and adult.

- Talking about sex with adults may feel uncomfortable to lesbian youth at times.

- It's always ok to decline to talk about sex; give lesbian youth this permission, too.

5. WANTING/NOT WANTING SEX

LEARN

Like other couples, some lesbian couples find their sexual interest wanes over time. While this may not be true for all lesbian couples, it is a situation lesbian couples do encounter.

PRACTICE

- Teach teens about the many different ways people experience sexuality.

- Among them are those people for whom sex holds no appeal.

- Asexual individuals are considered a natural human variation in sexual interest.

- Offer acceptance and validation for this way of being.

- On the other hand, slut shaming in North American cultures leads lesbian youth who desire sexual relations to feel ashamed. The shame itself is extremely damaging to both the personality structure of lesbian youth, as well as their ability to relate to others.

- Make an effort to tease out the presence of slut shaming in lesbian youth.

REFLECT

- In American hypersexualized culture, youth are exposed to more sexual content than ever before. For asexual lesbian youth, validating their lack of interest in sex offers a protective factor for their emerging identity.

- For lesbian youth with sexual desires, it's very important to reinforce the healthy nature of wanting sex. Countering cultural influences is important for other females and non-binary youth; however, it's particularly important for personality and sexual development in lesbian youth.

6. ATTRACTION, DATING, AND COMMUNITY

LEARN

Lesbian youth often experience invisibility, and as such, dating and finding partners can be a challenge. Finding yourself attracted to another girl, and not knowing if she's into girls can make it hard to pair up, or even talk about it.

PRACTICE

Here are some tips to consider if you find yourself attracted to another girl, and you're not sure if she's open to it or not:

- **Begin slowly:** Ask general questions like: "Do you have a crush on anyone?" Or, "Who do you think is cute?" Another option is: "Are you into anyone these days?"

- **Raise the topic:** Inquire about current events in the news that pertain to LGBTQ+ youth to gauge their interest and open mindedness about the topic. Discuss marriage equality, Gay Straight Alliance in schools, etc.

- **Set boundaries with inappropriate stuff:** If you hear an offensive joke, try to speak up and say it's not ok to make jokes like that in front of you. Try to stand up for others if you hear homophobic comments, though don't be hard on yourself if you can't.
It's really tough stuff!

- **Use media, entertainment, movies, and music:** Discuss shows, music, and other entertainment that includes lesbian characters. Notice how your friend reacts when you bring up scenes or songs about females loving females. You can use this topic as a jumping off point to bring up girls kissing girls, and see how your friend feels about it.

- **Ask another friend:** If there is someone else at your school who is out as a lesbian, mention their name to your friend. Notice their reaction. Alternatively, you can go to that person and ask if they know if the girl you like might be open to it. Sometimes friends know things that other people do not.

- **Be brave!** If you feel comfortable, you can try the direct approach and ask: "Are you gay?" You can also drop hints that you're interested in girls.

REFLECT

- It can be hard to broach the topic of sex and dating.

- Stop talking about this topic if you, or your friend, becomes uncomfortable. You can say: "I know I brought this up, but it's really hard for me. Maybe we can talk about it another time."

- It's important to avoid directly asking people about their sexual orientation unless you have a close relationship already. People can get really embarrassed, and feel outed even though that wasn't your intention.

- It can be hard to find the right time to talk to someone about sexuality and attraction. Find a private place.

- Finding people who are like you can be a little challenging. It just means you need to look in places like the GSA, the gay and lesbian center in your community, or new friend groups. You can do it!

SLEEPOVERS AND PARENTS

LEARN

Parents often feel more comfortable with same gender sleepovers in adolescence. This tends to result from the fear that heterosexual hookups can lead to pregnancy and STD transmission. When parents learn about their daughter being lesbian, a same gender sleepover can cause conflict between lesbian youth and parents.

PRACTICE

Tips for lesbian youth to use when dealing with parents:

- Reassure your parents that the door will always be open to your room.

- Tell your parents that you respect them and that you are honorable. Then stick to it.

- If you really want your girlfriend to sleep over and it makes your parents uncomfortable, find the compromise where nobody is happy. Agree to be in open sight and don't fool around, or just sleep separately. At least you two can be nearer to each other.

REFLECT

- Negotiating parental rules and limits around sex and dating is challenging for youth, maybe more so for lesbian youth because the social structure doesn't support their development.

- See if you can balance your needs with your parents' rules. It's hard, but if you care about them and yourself at the same time, you can find the middle path.

8. "LOTS OF LESBIANS PLAY ELITE SPORTS" (ZIEGLER, 2016)

LEARN

Two weeks before Jason Collins came out, WNBA star Brittney Griner came out. She received much less media attention.

WNBA TV revenue is $10 million compared to the NBA's $2.67 billion per year.

Many lesbian athletes came out earlier, such as Sheryl Swoopes in 2005, and the consensus among WNBA players was that it's easier to count straight players than lesbians.

Ziegler disagrees with this consensus. From his perspective as a gay sports journalist, there is a preponderance of lesbians in elite-level team sports.

For lesbian youth, athletes also serve as civil rights activists who've paved the way for coming out and being authentic. (This is also true for gay, bisexual, and transyouth, too.)

PRACTICE

- As part of your development into adulthood, your sexual identity is a critical element. Learning about the lesbian athletes who are out there is one way to find role models that empower and inspire you.

- Read up about tennis pro Martina Navratilova, tennis pro Billie Jean King, pro soccer player Abby Wambach and her new wife Glennon Doyle.

REFLECT

- Athlete Ally is a nonprofit organization promoting LGBTQ+ allies in athletics.

9. EARLY CHILDHOOD SEXUAL EXPERIMENTATION

LEARN

Some lesbians have had early sexual experiences in their childhood. The urge, curiosity, and interest in exploring sex is totally normal and doesn't necessarily appear for the first time in the teen years. For some, messing around in childhood is quite common and need not be associated with shame—especially if both people consented.

PRACTICE

This practice is an invitation to give yourself permission to move beyond any childhood sexual experiences that leave you feeling shameful.

There's nothing more to this practice than letting go and allowing yourself to be perfectly human with all the positive and negative experiences that come with the ride. Try it now.

REFLECT

- Letting go is much easier said than done. If you find this practice challenging, just know it's ok! It's common.

- Take your time with letting go. Sit with the idea for a while without committing to it.

- If any part of your childhood experiences felt traumatic or violating, they probably were. Letting go may be much harder in these situations. Take the time to heal the experience in order to let it go. Rely on professional help to do so because it's pretty hard stuff.

Gay Youth

Male gender role expectations influence identity development in gay youth. Sexual health and the impact of the HIV crisis endure in the gay community, and therefore, they deserve some elucidation as gay youth develop. With substance use also a concern in the gay community, it can be assessed using Substance Abuse Self-Test in Appendix D.

1. MEN WHO LOVE MEN

LEARN

For gay youth, self-esteem and relationship skills are intertwined with homophobia and internalized homophobia (Edwards & Sylaska, 2012). Gay youth are at particular risk for problems in their developing identity and capacity for intimacy.

For gay youth to develop a healthy sense of self, some clarity is needed about identity, relationships, and exposure to positive gay role models.

Regretfully, the word "gay" is used negatively in society. To identify oneself as "gay" means to automatically confront and struggle with stereotypes, even placing oneself in a category of oppressed people. This leads to problems with identity formation, which can also lead to intimacy problems.

Role models, acceptance, and a wide range of stories contribute to a healthy and positive sense of self. It also leads to the capacity for positive intimacy development. When society obstructs positive identity development in gay youth, dysfunctional relationships can be expected to develop for those men.

PRACTICE

Examine the words/phrases and see if you've ever been affected by any of them:

- Sissy
- Wimp
- Different
- Not manly enough
- Not assertive/aggressive enough
- Not a real man
- Girly
- The absence of positive gay role models
- Few dating norms for gay teens
- Lack of acceptance of normal "crushes" and infatuations
- Non-judgmental information regarding sexual curiosity
- Paternal acceptance

- Lack of expected male bonding due to homophobia
- Acceptable male friendships and relationships
- Predator
- Unsuitable for the "hard professions"
- Unable to form mature non-erotic relationships
- Useless, if not harmful, to the survival of the race
- Criminal seducers
- Misogynist
- Immature and victims of pathological development
- Sexually disordered
- The cause of crime in the streets
- The cause of AIDS
- God hates fags

REFLECT

- Explore and discuss your experiences with these phrases/words.
- If it is too difficult to discuss, you can journal about it, or just sit silently with it.
- There is great power in being able to sit silently with difficult and troubling matters.

BEING MANLY AND LOVING

LEARN

Loving and nurturing others is coded feminine and soft in North American culture. For males to choose to love each other involves embracing the union of the masculine and feminine parts, while also rejecting social norms.

PRACTICE

In the space provided, write down and release all the stereotypes you hold about:

Being male/masculine – conforming to male stereotypes:

_____
_____
_____

Being female/feminine – begin gender expansive:

_____
_____
_____

Being agender/bigender/pangender – not conforming to male stereotypes:

_____
_____
_____

REFLECT

- It's ok to acknowledge how social and cultural stereotypes influence you.

- Sexuality and attraction aren't necessarily tied to society and culture, even though both can have strong influences. The purpose of examining the influence of stereotypes on you is to tease out and release any that hold you back. If there aren't any, that's awesome!

3. GAY SEX AND SAFETY

LEARN

Unfortunately, the HIV/AIDS crisis hit the gay community the hardest and struck strong association. For gay youth, this may include the burden of this stigma attached to sex. The degree to which you acknowledge this issue and practice safe sex can not only influence your health and well-being, but also release you from the stigma. Facing something strengthens *you*, while hiding from it strengthens *it*.

PRACTICE

- Discover the current rates of HIV/AIDS in the gay community.

- Explore safe sexual practices, including consent and intimate partner violence in the gay community.

- Practice safe sex always, including receiving full overt and verbal consent from your partner.

REFLECT

- It's important for gay youth to be informed about the association between their community and HIV/AIDS.

- Exploring difficult topics early on keeps them from becoming sources of shame, and thriving in secrecy, silence, and judgment. It promotes healthy sexual identity formation.

4. COMMUNITY BELONGING

LEARN

Social belonging is a fundamental human need. Just one instance of exclusion could impact functioning and long-term outcomes. For gay youth, it is extremely important to find belonging with others.

PRACTICE

- Find your local gay and lesbian center/GSA so you can hang out with others.

- If one is not available in your area/school, consider beginning a GSA at school.

- If that's not your thing at this time, it's ok! Here's something you can say to yourself to get through the challenging moments when you feel like you might not belong:

> *I am not all alone, even when I feel that way.*
>
> *There are others who feel just like me. This situation will change.*

REFLECT

- Remembering the interconnectedness of all beings comes in handy in moments of aloneness.

- It's also important to nurture real life connections with others.

5. BODY IMAGE

LEARN

Gay culture places emphasis on physical shape. Growing up gay male is tough enough with discrimination, harassment, and parental rejection in some instances! Body Dysmorphic Disorder (BDD) occurs when a person is so dissatisfied with their physical body that they take drastic steps to change it. This problem affects females and males equally; however, it impacts the gay community fairly frequently.

PRACTICE

Just self-reflect for a moment, and see how concerned you are about the following parts of the body:

- Muscle tone and definition
- Six pack abdominals
- Nice hair
- Attractive face
- Great style
- Make-up
- Hiding skin flaws and blemishes

Next, if there are any areas above that really bug you, please circle them.

Then rate how much it is a problem for you from 0-10, where 0 = no problem, and 10 = HUGE PROBLEM. Write the number next to the items you circled.

REFLECT

- It takes strength, courage, and bravery to face your issues.
- If your issues include focusing on your physical body in some way, please take this moment to send yourself some loving kindness.

Bisexual Youth

Understanding bisexuality as a legitimate and distinct identity remains a crucial concern that impacts youth who love males, females, and more. For our purposes, this chapter pertains mainly to bisexual youth; however, pansexual, omnisexual, polysexual, and polyamorous youth experience some of the same things too, and are referred to wherever appropriate. The harmfulness of bisexual erasure is explored in this chapter, with activities and practices designed to promote embracing bisexual identity with joy.

1. CREATING COMMUNITY

LEARN

A bisexual person can be attracted to male, female, and even non-binary individuals. Research demonstrates that almost half of the LGBTQ+ population identifies as bisexual. Even though bi people make up more than half the LGBTQ+ population, invisibility and erasure are among the primary issues faced in the bisexual community. Advocates are working to change the visibility of bi individuals. In the meantime, use the form below to explore your needs for interacting with other bi youth.

PRACTICE

Do you know any other people/teens who are bi/pansexual? If so, how did you meet and do you interact them on a regular basis?

_____
_____
_____

Is it important to you that other people know you are bi/pansexual? Is it important to you to interact with other bi/pansexual people?

_____
_____
_____

Where/how might you find and interact with other bi/pansexual teens?

_____
_____
_____

REFLECT

- It isn't necessarily important to all bi/pansexual teens to interact with others like them.

- It's ok if you do not have the need.

- If you do need community with others like you, please seek it out. The questions above just help clarify whether this need exists or not.

2. FINDING VALUE IN DIFFERENCES

LEARN

The gay community is made up of a rainbow of diverse members. It includes lesbians and transpeople, as well as pangender, agender, and bi/pansexual people, too. For bi/pansexual youth, the need to celebrate differences, as well as their rightful existence, can be an important part of identity development. The absence of role models can create tension as young people come into bi/pansexual identity. The reflective questions below clarify the uniqueness of being bi/pansexual.

PRACTICE

List all the beautiful aspects of being bi/pansexual:

- _____
- _____
- _____
- _____
- _____
- _____
- _____

- _____
- _____
- _____
- _____
- _____
- _____
- _____

List all the ways being bi/pansexual differs from being gay/lesbian and how it works for you:

- _____
- _____
- _____
- _____
- _____
- _____

- _____
- _____
- _____
- _____
- _____
- _____

REFLECT

- This can be a very private reflection; you need not share with anyone else.

- The practice of exploring the unique and beautiful parts of being bi/pansexual is in itself the best part. Please enjoy it for the moment.

3. DOUBLE DISCRIMINATION

LEARN

Being bi, or even pansexual, can leave you feeling alienated and alone. It's hard to fit in with lesbian teens, gay teens, and straight ones, too. Some bi (or pansexual youth) feel like they aren't welcome in the gay/lesbian communities because they are open to loving a wide range of people. Facing discrimination from within the LGBTQ+ community, as well as the dominant culture, is called Double Discrimination. Let's take a moment to look at this and see if it impacts you.

PRACTICE

Have there been times when you tried to interact with others who are gay and found yourself not so welcome? Please reflect on that time for a moment, then write about it here if you feel comfortable.

_____
_____
_____

If you could replay the scene once more and re-live it, is there anything you might do differently?

_____
_____
_____

If you could give any message to gay/lesbian allies about being bi or pansexual, what would it be? Imagine they would receive your message with the heartfelt sincerity offered, and that they would totally get it too!

_____
_____
_____

REFLECT

- Not all bi (pansexual) youth experience exclusion from within the LGBTQ+ community. It's ok if you are not exposed to this.

- The questions above assist bi (pansexual) youth in discovering the diversity within the LGBTQ+ community and coping with the discrimination they may face as a result.

4. COPING WITH ERASURE

LEARN

One of the challenges of being bi/pansexual is that you don't fit neatly into the predominant LGBTQ+ identities. Lesbian and gay teens sometimes exclude bi/pansexual youth as not fully out of the closet and identifying with their authentic lesbian/gay nature. This way of being and dismissing bi/pansexual identity as legitimate is called bi/pansexual erasure. In response, many bi/pansexual youth further assert their love for all people, which falls on deaf ears. Explore the questions to see if bi/pansexual erasure is a concern for you.

PRACTICE

When you interact with straight friends, do you avoid telling them about the range of your sexual attraction? If yes, why? If not, how does it go?

_____
_____
_____
_____

When you are with lesbian and gay friends, do you tell them about your straight attractions and sexual experiences? If yes, how does it go? If not, why do you avoid it?

_____
_____
_____
_____

Is it easy for you to come out as bi? Why or why not?

_____
_____
_____
_____

Do you feel as well-received as if you were gay/lesbian/straight? Please explain.

_____

_____

_____

_____

_____

How do you cope when you feel left out or as if you don't belong anywhere?

_____

_____

_____

_____

_____

REFLECT

- Being your true self is different for everyone.

- It's ok if you feel well received and welcome in a variety of social circles—in fact, it's great news!

- For other bi/pansexual teens who find it hard to fit in and interact people like them, the practice is intended to strengthen self-compassion muscles and decrease suffering associated with exclusion.

Transgender and Intersex Identity Developement

Options for gender expression, gender expansiveness, and gender creative youth are explored in this chapter, along with definition of terms. (Not all who are gender expansive wish to transition, so some issues will be introduced here, and followed up in Chapter Seven on questioning youth.) Transphobia and internalized transphobia can complicate healthy gender identity development and/or transition, and are therefore explored here. The Gray Gender Spectrum integrates complexities about gender identity, expression, and bodies, while other practices assist professionals and youth in assessing the persistence, insistence, and consistency of gender dysphoria. Names, pronouns, body confidence, positivity, and self-love are explored in this chapter, too.

Gender Spectrum is an organization in Northern California providing support and educational programming for gender expansive youth and their families. Schools and other organizations turn to Gender Spectrum for professional development and other trainings. With appreciation for their leadership, creativity, and ability to serve the needs of gender creative individuals, two of their documents are referred to in this chapter, and located in Appendix F.

1. THE RAINBOW OF GENDER

LEARN

Gender is a social construct that extends way beyond the binary of male and female. Science tells us that gender may not even be a linear spectrum (Wu, 2016). Like other aspects of identity, it exists on a number of dimensions simultaneously, and seems to lie outside the scope of current systems of classification. Moreover, gender may not be as stable and unchanging over time as we assume.

PRACTICE

Since you probably already know most of this stuff, take this moment to practice sharing and educate the adult who gave this sheet to you. It's possible that this stuff may be newer to them than to you. By practicing sharing and educating with a trusted adult, you'll become better at it when you need to do it out in the world.

Explain the following terms to your adult caregiver:

- **AFAB:** **A**ssigned **F**emale **A**t **B**irth

- **AMAB:** **A**ssigned **M**ale **A**t **B**irth

- **Cisgender:** personal gender identity corresponds with gender identity assigned at birth

- **Non-Binary (NB):** neither male nor female, or maybe even both, or simply no association with gender. They can be AFAB or AMAB. Also known as **genderqueer** and **gender expansive youth**

- **Transgender:**
  - **Transfemale (MtF)**
  - **Transmale (FtM)**

- **Transition:** the process of medical and social transition from one gender to another. Binary transpeople go through a process ranging from name change, clothing and hair choices, hormone replacement therapy, surgery, and voice coaching in order to present as their authentic selves

- **HRT:** Hormone Replacement Therapy

- Surgeries

- Presenting differently

- Legal name change

- **Passing:** not read/seen as trans, or passing as cisgender, including physical gender cues, behavioral attributes, and mannerisms

If you feel open and comfortable, discuss any of the terms on the previous page as they pertain to you.

REFLECT

- It may seem unnecessary to practice reviewing the terms and concepts with your trusted adult. Unfortunately, there are many people who just don't know this stuff. You may find yourself faced with explaining basic concepts to people. Doing so with grace and kindness represents you, and the community, really well.

2. GENDER FLUIDITY

LEARN

Early theories and ideas about gender suggest it was tied to genitals, chromosomes, and either male or female. With progress, growth, and awareness, we now accept a wide range of genders, beyond the traditional binary of female and male. Gender identity refers to an internal psychological experience. For some people, labels don't apply.

For others, the gender assigned at birth does not apply. In the case of intersex individuals, there are 140 chromosomal conditions that lead to ambiguity in assumed gender. For these reasons, and so many more, youth today benefit from freedom to creatively explore gender. The practice below invites you and your trusted adult caregiver to explore the full range and fluidity that is gender.

PRACTICE

Explore the terms below. Define and explain whatever you know about them. If any are new to you, look them up on the internet and discover new things with your trusted adult.

- Male/masculine
- Female/feminine
- Androgynous/Androgyne
- Pangender
- Bigender
- Agender
- Two-spirit
- Third gender
- Fa'afafine
- Non-binary
- Gender expansive
- Transfemale/trans/MtF
- Transmale/trans/FtM
- Misogyny/transmisogyny/misogynoir

REFLECT

- Find the answer key with definitions to the words above in Chapter One, Activity #2.
- Some terms may be obvious and others perhaps new and unfamiliar.
- Try to remain open to learning something new, even about terms that you've known about your whole life or feel expert about.

3. THE GRAY GENDER SPECTRUM

LEARN

As established earlier, gender identity seems to fall on a spectrum. Look below to see the different shades of gray, I mean gender, that fall between the black and white of the gender binary. Keep in mind that gender is expressed in a variety of ways, for example: the body, identity, and even the style, names, pronouns, and mannerisms used to present publicly (Brill & Kenney, 2016).

Use the grid below to explore your gender "identity" and "expression," as well as your "body." You can place a check mark in the box that corresponds to the category under "gender" - if any fit. Alternatively, you can write a little in the boxes that feel relevant to you - or not. Remember to explore the bottom rows of the grid to see if there are any differences between your "past," "present," and/or "ideal" gender "identity," "expression," and/or "body."

PRACTICE

Gender	Body	Identity	Expression
Totally female/feminine			
Mostly female/feminine			
A mix of female/feminine & male/masculine			
Mostly male/masculine			
Totally male/masculine			
Neither female/feminine nor male/masculine			
	Past	Present	Ideal

REFLECT

- Explore the gray areas of gender. Where do you fall on the Gray Gender Spectrum?

- How is it for you to identify most authentically? Does it come easily?

- How might you embrace your authentic nature and express your gender identity in a way that most represents your true heart?

4. GENDER DYSPHORIA

LEARN

Gender dysphoria happens to some people early in life, to others later in life, and to some not at all. It's the experience of feeling very unhappy, as if born in the body of the wrong gender, and/or assigned the wrong gender at birth regardless of body parts.

Gender dysphoria comes with a clear knowing about one's gender and a strong misalignment with their body. This misalignment is so strong as to cause great depression and self-loathing. Coupled with society's lack of acceptance of gender expansive people, it's downright hard to resolve gender dysphoria.

There are three aspects of gender dysphoria that are assessed to determine if a person is ready and eligible to transition:

- Insistence
- Persistence
- Consistency

PRACTICE

The following questionnaire is intended to assess how insistent, persistent, and consistent your gender dysphoria is.

REFLECT

- Please share the results of this short questionnaire with a trusted adult.
- You deserve all the support in being your true Self. Keep going for that and finding people who help you along the way.

GENDER DYSPHORIA SCALE

Rate the following statements on a scale of 1-7:

1	2	3	4	5	6	7
Not at all			**Somewhat**			**Totally**

1. I feel terrible when I look at my genitals. _____

2. I wish my parents let me wear clothes of another gender. _____

3. When I think about the gender I was assigned at birth, I get so hopeless. _____

4. I wish everyone knew my true gender. _____

5. I would be so much happier if I was another gender. _____

6. I would take measures (hormones, legal name change, surgery) to change myself/my body to better align with my gender. _____

7. Sometimes I feel like I am not even in my body, but rather outside looking in. _____

8. Life feels like a dream; this "reality" doesn't feel real at all. _____

9. Changing my body to affirm my authentic gender would make me much happier. _____

10. I avoid going out because I can't be seen as my true self. _____

11. My life is worse off because of the gender I was assigned at birth. _____

12. I think about killing myself because my body and the gender I was assigned at birth don't match my sense of Self. _____

13. I've felt this way for a little while. _____

14. This way of life has been with me for so long I can't remember a time it wasn't like this. _____

15. My gender is clear to me. Why can't others get it? _____

Copyright © 2018 Lee-Anne Gray. *LGBTQ+ Youth*. All rights reserved.

5. IS IT A BODY IMAGE PROBLEM OR THE GENDER?

LEARN

There are a few different ways to look at gender and/or body image concerns. One way to look at this dilemma is that a person was assigned the wrong gender at birth and feels like they are in the wrong body. This often leads to negative experiences. In another case, a person could feel like they were assigned the right gender at birth, but that their body isn't quite right or pleasing. How do you know which it is? Here's how to figure it out.

PRACTICE

	Gender Dysphoria	Body Dysmorphic
Body concerns	Related to gender	May be stereotyped along gender lines, but are not related to gender
Internal sense of gender	Misalignment between body and assigned gender at birth	Alignment between body and gender assignment at birth
Desired outcome	Name, body, and gender change	Improved physical appearance along cultural norms and standards
Insight	May be present and clear	May be good/fair/poor or absent and delusional

REFLECT

- There's a big difference between body dysmorphic disorder and gender dysphoria. For transyouth, transitioning improves lives, health, well-being, and functioning. For those with body dysmorphic disorder, bodily improvements aren't commonly associated with improved functioning.

- Knowing this difference may help you advocate for yourself.

6. NAMES AND PRONOUNS

LEARN

Your name and the pronouns used to talk with you, and about you, are important to your identity! It can be rough when you need to correct people and let them know they've made a mistake in assuming your gender. The following practice is intended to help you find the words when you need to advocate for yourself.

PRACTICE

Write your chosen name:

_____

Write your preferred pronouns:

_____

Create a few sample statements you might use to inform someone about your chosen name and preferred pronouns. Just put some words down, even if they don't seem to make sense. Getting the imperfect words out is one way to discover what you want to say and what you don't want to say.

- _____
- _____
- _____
- _____
- _____
- _____
- _____
- _____

REFLECT

- It's ok if at first the phrases you come up with don't work. It's expected.
- Keep trying to find new ways of saying whatever works for you.
- Invite assistance from a trusted friend or adult, if you can.

7. BEAUTY IN NON-BINARY BODIES

LEARN

Beautiful bodies come in all shapes and sizes and extend way beyond societal norms. For young people with gender non-conforming bodies, it's important to find ways to love the skin you're in and the body that carries your soul.

PRACTICE

In the lines below, list all the things you could love about yourself. You don't have to be perfect, nor fit social norms. Just list a few things you like about your body even if it isn't perfect.

_____

_____

_____

_____

_____

_____

_____

REFLECT

- Loving non-binary bodies is an act of self-preservation and also a civil rights statement.

- When you find just one thing to cherish in your body that may not conform to your authentic gender, you're practicing self-kindness and self-compassion. Combined together, they lead people to finding more ways of enjoying themselves and the lives they live—even when life is hard.

8. TRANSPHOBIA, INTERNALIZED TRANSPHOBIA, AND SELF-ACCEPTANCE

LEARN

Transphobia is a spectrum of negative attitudes toward transpeople. It can include disgust, fear, violence, and/or anger towards people who do not conform to gender norms. This manifests in several ways:

- Subtle and/or overt discrimination and oppression
- Emphasis on cisnormativity, cisgenderism, and/or cissexuality

When transpeople align with transphobic values—even in subtle or unconscious ways—it can be called internalized transphobia. It's challenging to track internalized transphobia because it looks like insidious self-loathing, which many people have. When it relates specifically to being trans or their transbody, then it may be internalized transphobia.

Ultimately, self-love and self-acceptance are the best remedies for anything transphobic, and they can arise through self-compassion practices, such as the one offered below.

PRACTICE

When any kind of hatred flows your way, whether from the outside in, or simmering within, try the Along With Me meditation (Gray, 2016).

When settled, silently look at the people around the room, or picture people in your mind, and for each person, say:

"Along with me, _____ wants to be happy." (Fill in the blank with the name of the person you are looking at, or imagining in your mind's eye.)

"Along with me _____ wants to be free of harm."

"Along with me, _____ wishes to be happy and safe."

- It is also beneficial to focus on just one person, and to repeat the phrases several times.
- Ideally, this activity would be introduced and practiced during moments of calm centeredness, to be called on during moments when internal or external loathing arises.

REFLECT

- Along With Me meditation is one way to be compassionate, and strengthen and center yourself in the face of hatred.

9. INTERSEX IDENTITY DEVELOPMENT

LEARN

According to Alice Dreger (2016), intersex infants were historically mistreated by the medical community. Born with ambiguous genitalia, intersex infants challenged physicians who assigned gender based on external characteristics. One strategy used decades ago was for surgeons to modify intersex infant genitalia so that gender could be assigned.

Unfortunately, this didn't turn out to be such a great solution. You probably already know this by now; gender isn't tied to genitals, so the surgery didn't necessarily align gender and body. For some intersex people who were treated this way, they grew up feeling like transpeople born in the wrong body/assigned the wrong gender at birth.

PRACTICE

- If you feel awkward about your gender and body, and have some questions—ask!

- It can be super hard to do so; however, opening the discussion may reveal things you need to know.

- Less than 2 percent of people are born with ambiguous genitalia (Fausto-Sterling, 2000), so this condition is rare.

- If infants have had surgeries to address the ambiguousness, sometimes intersex individuals disappear in the gender binary.

- Asking questions about your body, gender, and any previous surgeries could lead to new discoveries in a few rare situations.

REFLECT

- Since being born intersex is really rare, it's unlikely to be the cause of gender expansiveness and transness.

- On the other hand, intersex is a real gender issue that is often ignored and surgically erased.

- Being aware of this element of gender and body enriches our collective sense of what gender really is.

Gender Transition

This chapter is intended to promote collaboration between clinicians and youth in assessing need/desire for gender transition. Worksheets are guided by the World Professional Association for Transgender Health (WPATH) Harry Benjamin Standards of Care (7th revision), so clinicians can document with risk management in mind. This chapter shifts the process of transitioning from one where clinicians judge who gets to transition to one of collaboration, affirmation, empathy, and compassion for gender expansive youth.

1. WHICH ASPECTS OF TRANSITION APPEAL/DON'T APPEAL

LEARN

When considering transition, there are three components of the triadic therapeutic approach:

1. Real life experience:

   - Living life as one's authentic gender
   - Expressing gender in the ways that feel true to nature
   - Name change
   - Pronoun change

2. Hormone treatment:

   - **Puberty blockers:** suppress the onset of puberty by blocking the release of hormones that elicit testosterone/estrogen
   - **Androgen blockers:** suppress the hormones that naturally arise in the body
   - **Estrogen/testosterone:** infuses the body with hormones that produce secondary sex characteristics

3. Surgery:

   - **Top surgery:** for a transmale, top surgery is breast reconstruction. For a transfemale, it could be breast augmentation
   - **Bottom surgery:** for transfemales, many choose the procedure to construct a vaginal canal out of a penis. These surgeries are not as common for transmales as they are for transfemales. The surgeries for transmales can include testicular implants, urethroplasty, scrotoplasty, mons resection, and metoidioplasty, which is less invasive and more affordable than a vaginectomy. Vaginectomy involves removal of the vaginal lining and sealing the opening. It provides more support for pelvic organs, while eliminating vaginal discharge.
   - **Orchiectomy:** removal of testicles only, leaving the penis alone
   - **Chondrolaryngoplasty** (commonly called tracheal shave): smoothes out the Adam's apple on the neck of transfemales

The 3 ways of transitioning described above are influenced by the Triadic Therapeutic Approach in the Standards of Care. There are 2 more associated terms to be familiar with:

- Social Transition
- Medical Transition

Social Transition refers to #1: "Real Life Experience"

Medical Transition refers to #2 and #3: "Hormones" and "Surgical body modification."

PRACTICE

- Evaluate the triadic therapeutic approach.

- Which aspects appeal to you, and which do not?

- Contemplate and consider the ramifications of the different parts of the triad.

- Some people feel kids and teens can't know if they should transition or not because they are still growing and changing. Do you ever feel this way? It's ok to explore this topic and know it can change over time.

REFLECT

- The process of transition looks very different for each person.

- Ultimately, the goal is to come to a place of self-love and authentic gender expression.

- Open to the possibility that your unique path to transition/or not will present itself to you as you continue to explore it.

2. READINESS TO TRANSITION

LEARN

When a person decides they are ready to transition, it can involve a series of steps and events. For instance, the medical doctor who prescribes hormone treatments may require a letter of readiness, or affirmation, from a mental health professional before beginning treatment. The current practice around transition letters is moving away from the mental health professional being a gatekeeper of transitioning, but rather a collaborator with kids and teens seeking transition. In the collaboration, seek to identify:

- Persistence
- Consistency
- Insistence

In joining with kids and teens to document transition readiness, mental health professionals need to assess the *persistent* nature of gender expansive presentations. Notice if it's been going on *consistently*, and how much they *insist* on being another gender.

Explore **Eligibility** & **Readiness:**

- **Eligibility** occurs when a person moves through the triadic therapeutic approach in the linear way. First, *living real life* as the other gender. Next, receiving *hormone treatment* before being **eligible** for surgery.

- **Readiness** is assessed using clinical judgment and may vary between individuals. Kids and teens can progress through treatment without the linear progression of real life experience, hormones, and then surgery last—if clinical judgment suggests otherwise.

When evaluating **readiness**, consider the severity of gender dysphoria and the presence of suicidality.

PRACTICE

The following is a template of a readiness letter reflecting the World Professional Association of Transgender Health (WPATH) and Harry Benjamin International Association's The Standards of Care (7th revision) for Gender Identity Disorders.

REFLECT

- One letter is required for hormone treatment

- Two separate letters from mental health professionals are required for surgery. One letter may come from the person's primary therapist. If the primary therapist has a master's degree, the second letter needs to be authored by someone with a doctoral or medical degree. If the first letter comes from a psychotherapist, the second letter can be authored by someone playing an evaluative role. One letter with two signatures also suffices the standards.

READINESS LETTER

To Whom It May Concern:

_____(state person's name, identifying characteristics such as: age, date of birth, race, ethnicity, nationality, sexual orientation, etc...) was assigned _____ (include gender assigned at birth) at birth, and has been evolving in their gender expression.

Throughout the course of my treatment with _____(include person's name) the following diagnoses have been rendered _____ (state diagnoses, if any; Gender Dysphoria should be included.). Currently, these diagnoses are _____ (state if they are ongoing conditions, in remission, re-classified with a different diagnosis, and/or if the severity of symptoms have changed.). The duration of treatment spans _____(insert date when treatment began), is ongoing, and consists of _____(state type of psychotherapy/number of sessions per week or all together.). The following evaluations were conducted: _____ (List the type of assessments, the date of assessment, and the assessor's name. If you are the assessor, state so. If there aren't any evaluations/assessments, include a statement about why there aren't any or simply that there aren't any at this time.).

To date, _____ (insert name of person) has met the following eligibility criteria _____ (state if the person has a) lived as their authentic gender, b) has taken hormone treatment/puberty blockers, and/or c) had any surgeries.).

In my professional opinion, _____'s (insert person's name) ability to follow the Standards of Care, particularly around medical after care is _____ (state: poor/fair/adequate/good/excellent.). They have the following sources of support: _____ (name any and all sources of support including private family, friends, public assistance and organizations.). My care of _____ (insert person's name) includes the following other members of the gender team: _____ (name all the people you consult and collaborate with in treating this person. If not working with a gender team, state so.). Please feel free to call me at _____ (include a telephone number where you can be reached directly) to verify the authenticity of the letter.

Sincerely and kindly,

_____
(your name)

3. GENDER SUPPORT AND TRANSITION PLANS

LEARN

Our friends at Gender Spectrum have created two sets of forms to support transitioning youth. The Gender Support Plan is a document that creates a shared understanding of how a student's authentic gender will be recorded in school documents. When used in collaboration with school staff, the Gender Support Plan eases transition, improves team communication, and reduces instances of discrimination.

The Gender Transition Plan is another document that shares information about youth transition, so that they can do so in a healthy, supportive environment.

PRACTICE

The Gender Support Plan and Gender Transition Plan can both be found in Appendix F. There is another document in Appendix F that assist in talking about gender and transgender students.

REFLECT

- The documents created by Gender Spectrum represent leading-edge communication templates for supporting gender-creative youth.

- Please support Gender Spectrum in any way you can – their work saves lives and helps us do our work more effectively.

 4. GENDER AFFIRMATION

LEARN

Gender identity and expression take on many different forms. For some people, transitioning is an important part of their gender affirmation and expression. For others, it is not. In the following practice, explore the varied and many details that you feel affirm/would affirm your gender identity.

PRACTICE

- Take a deep breath, allowing the air to pass through your nostrils, filling your lungs and belly.

- Feel your body and take a moment to scan it for any tingling, tightness, or other sensations. Just notice your body and gender, and make contact with them in this very moment.

- Next, allow yourself to consider all the different ways you want to present your gender in the world, and be seen by others.

- Allow the thoughts, images, and feelings about it to float into your awareness.

- Take a few minutes to rest quietly in this space, allowing different aspects of gender identity and presentation to come to consciousness.

- When you're ready, take a deep cleansing breath, open your eyes, and return to the room.

- Now, take a pen (or an electronic device) and write down everything that came to mind, and/or continues to come to mind.

REFLECT

- This practice invites you to become more intimate with yourself. It leads to greater ease and familiarity with needs and wants.

- It's ok if some uncomfortable ideas, memories, or thoughts come to you. Try to let them go, and focus back on the task at hand.

- If the discomfort is too great or persists, talk with someone you trust.

5. DEVELOPMENTAL GENDER AND CHRONOLOGICAL GENDER

LEARN

For transpeople, awareness of the difference between assigned gender at birth and authentic gender identity can happen at any time in life. For some, it is known early and strongly. For others, the awareness comes a little later on, say the teen years or adulthood.

- **Chronological Gender** is how long you've been living with the gender you were assigned at birth.

- **Developmental Gender** is how long you've been living as your authentic self. This refers to people who are/have actively and outwardly began their transition. Some people are trans or non-binary and don't transition for a wide range of reasons. This concept is more narrow in its application to transpeople who have and are outwardly transitioning.

The practice below reflects these different stages of gender identity development. See where you're at!

PRACTICE

How old are you? _____

This is your *chronological gender*.

How long ago did you transition? _____

This is your *developmental gender*. It corresponds to transition, not the moment you realized you're trans.

REFLECT

- Explore the different ages of your chronological and developmental gender.

- See if one feels more true, and/or if one feels less different.

- Looking at chronological and developmental gender identity ages facilitates the integration of self. It is one step towards noticing where you're at, and where you've been. It's also a mindfulness practice to become aware of nuances and details about yourself.

- Remember some transpeople go through puberty more than once. It's ok if your chronological and developmental gender ages are wide apart.

6. ASSESSMENT OF LEVEL OF DISTRESS ASSOCIATED WITH GENDER ASSIGNED AT BIRTH

LEARN
One of the critical aspects to consider when thinking about transitioning is how much distress you feel about your gender, your body, and the gender you were assigned at birth.

PRACTICE
Thinking about the following aspects of your identity, rate your distress level from 0-10 (0 = no distress at all; 10 = so much distress that you even think about killing yourself sometimes):

My body:

← -- →

0   1   2   3   4   5   6   7   8   9   10

My authentic gender:

← -- →

0   1   2   3   4   5   6   7   8   9   10

My gender assigned at birth:

← -- →

0   1   2   3   4   5   6   7   8   9   10

REFLECT
- It's ok to admit you're suffering, and that it has profound effects on you.

- The trusted adult who gave this to you is here to help. Turn to them with the distress you feel so you can get the support and relief you deserve.

- Oftentimes, transitioning helps ease the distress transpeople feel around their body and gender identity.

- It's important to look at how much distress and suffering is going on. When suicide is in the mix, transitioning could be a better option.

7. VARIATIONS IN GENDER EXPRESSION

LEARN

Gender expression varies among people. It varies in different cultures, too! When transgender people think about transitioning, gender expression is at the forefront. You can practice different forms of gender expression at any time, without committing to transition. It's ok to explore, and maybe you already have.

PRACTICE

1. Which aspects of gender expression appeal to you?

   _____
   _____
   _____
   _____

2. Do you like any aspects of the gender you were assigned at birth?

   _____
   _____
   _____
   _____

3. Which aspects of no gender appeal to you?

   _____
   _____
   _____
   _____

4. Do any aspects of expressing another gender appeal to you? If so, what are they?

_____

_____

_____

_____

5. Have you experimented with different forms of gender expression? If so, how did it go?

_____

_____

_____

_____

6. Have you had positive/negative/neutral experiences exploring your gender identity and expressing it? If so, what were they?

_____

_____

_____

_____

REFLECT

- You can explore the questions with someone you trust, or keep it to yourself.

- Remember, it's also an act of self-compassion to become aware of yourself and bring kindness to that knowing.

Questioning Youth

Gender and sexuality can feel rigid and defined, especially in North American culture. Questioning youth remind us that this is an illusion. Chapter Seven explores fluidity and openness to both gender and sexuality. It offers youth and clinicians/educators an opportunity to explore sexual and gender identity with openness and without the need to label.

1. GENDER FLUIDITY

LEARN

Some young people feel most authentic without labeling their gender, while others feel the need to take on new labels to better express themselves. Whether you're figuring things out about your gender or are absolutely certain, just know it's ok to be however you want! Genderqueer, agender, bigender, pangender, and other terms are separate ways to express gender expansiveness or non-conformity. In the practice below, evaluate your queerness, for you. Just look at how fluid your gender feels, or not. Remember, it can change over time; it can also be stable over time. Everyone is different, and change happens.

PRACTICE

(0 = not at all; 10 = totally)

1. When thinking about your gender identity, how much does it match the one you were assigned at birth?

    ← -- →
    0   1   2   3   4   5   6   7   8   9   10

2. When thinking about the binary terms for gender (male/female,) how much do they apply to you?

    ← -- →
    0   1   2   3   4   5   6   7   8   9   10

3. When imagining how you'd like to be seen by others, how well do the binary gender terms fit you?

    ← -- →
    0   1   2   3   4   5   6   7   8   9   10

4. Do you feel more gender expansive than the binary terms allow? If so, discuss how much.

    ← -- →
    0   1   2   3   4   5   6   7   8   9   10

REFLECT

- Going beyond the gender binary means you embrace gender fluidity and/or expansiveness.

- It's ok if this leaves you feeling different. Most people feel different in some way, especially LGBTQ+ youth still figuring it all out.

2. SEXUAL FLUIDITY

LEARN

Another way youth can be questioning is around sexuality. Experimenting and identifying as anything other than straight can involve a process of coming to awareness and out to others. The following practice invites you to consider sexuality beyond the obvious straight/heteronormative and being open to any possibility that fits you.

PRACTICE

Explore the terms for sexuality:

- Pansexual
- Bisexual
- Omnisexual
- Skoliosexual
- Demisexual
- Grey Ace
- Asexual
- Polysexual

REFLECT

- Looking up the terms above, (or find definitions in the answer key in Chapter One) if any are unfamiliar to you; it could be one way to better understand yourself and your emerging sexuality.

- For some people, there is variation and fluidity throughout their lives. For other people, sexuality remains stable. Let yourself know who you are, whether it changes over time or not.

3. IMPERMANENCE

LEARN

In Buddhist psychology, we learn that so much is ever-changing—everything is impermanent! Questioning youth seem to understand this at a deep level while challenging the definitions of gender, sexuality, and what it means to be human.

PRACTICE

Anatta is the state of self that is ever-changing.

Consider the statement above.

To what extent do you/do you not identify with the changing nature of being human?

_____
_____
_____

Do you feel your gender and sexual identities are fixed, rigid, and exactly as you were assigned at birth? Discuss.

_____
_____
_____

Are the assumptions made about you, your gender, and/or your sexuality *always* accurate? Why/why not?

_____
_____
_____

Could there be parts of you that change and develop over time? If so, what, why, and how? If not, why?

_____

_____

_____

_____

In what ways are your gender identity and/or sexual orientation fluid and changing or fixed and rigid?

_____

_____

_____

_____

REFLECT

- It takes courage and bravery to question anything!

- That you're even taking this time to explore the variations in human nature, sexuality, and gender identity is a gift to you, and to the whole world!

- When you take this time to better know yourself, with kindness, and remembering that there are others like you, it transforms. You transform, your interactions become very different, and everyone around you starts to seem quite different, too.

4. GROWTH MINDSET AND NEUROPLASTICITY

LEARN

Research by Carol Dweck (2006) suggests that having a "growth" mindset contributes to greater success. This mindset embraces the idea of impermanence described in practice #3, and grounds it in research. We now know that the brain is plastic, and can generate new connections throughout life. With this in mind, people can definitely grow and change. They can cultivate new talents, skills, and abilities simply by being open and practicing.

When it comes to questioning youth, it's like the growth mindset is already in action. The days of "fixed" mindset are long gone; the genes and intelligence we are born with aren't simply what we get—it can be so much more over time! Similarly, the gender assigned at birth, and the sexuality we are assumed to have may change over time, and/or not be fixed at all.

PRACTICE

Fixed mindset:

How do you feel about change?

_____

_____

_____

_____

How do you feel about stagnation? Has your personal style ever stagnated, stalled, or just gotten plain stuck?

_____

_____

_____

_____

Growth mindset:

In what ways are you open to and embracing change?

_____

_____

_____

What aspects of change excite you?

___

Which parts of change are frightening or worth avoiding?

___

Gender and/or sexuality:

When you consider your gender and/or sexuality, which mindset applies best? Fixed or growth, and why?

___

REFLECT

- Remember, there are no right or wrong answers, and no "correct" way to be.

- Being you can change over time as you figure out who you are, as well as what you need and want to thrive.

- Take all the time you need to explore your gender and sexuality. Whichever mindset you take, just be you!

PART II
Clinical Approaches to LGBTQ+ Youth Treatment

Introduction to Part II

In the next part of this book, the focus shifts from activities used directly with LGBTQ+ youth to those used on their behalf. Part II has a three-tiered approach to caring for LGBTQ+ youth:

1. **Individual**
2. **Family**
3. **Community**

The individual tier is addressed in **Chapters Eight and Nine, focusing on self-compassion, kindness for reactions, and compassion, as well as increased mindful awareness and empathic capacity for both professionals and the LGBTQ+ youth in their care.** In addition to addressing the internal experiences, implicit bias, and socialized stereotypes, the clinician/educator also needs tools to bring authentic acceptance and affirmation to the LGBTQ+ youth in their care. Just like professionals need self-compassion to cope with the demands of being caring professionals, LGBTQ+ youth also benefit from learning self-compassion practices.

Chapter Nine shows the clinician/educator how to safely train LGBTQ+ youth in self-compassion while mitigating risks. Moreover, the research demonstrates that family acceptance is correlated with improved outcomes for LGBTQ+ youth (Ryan et al., 2009; 2010; Grant et al., 2011; Newton, 2014; HRC, 2012), which leads to **Chapter 10 focusing on strategies for helping. Chapter 11 closes out Part II**, and this book, with social justice strategies that clinicians, educators, administrators, and parents can use to make schools safer for LGBTQ+ youth.

1. ECOLOGICAL SYSTEMS THEORY

LEARN

Bronfenbrenner's (1979) ecological systems theory suggests that people are part of interconnected and related systems, with the individual at the center. LGBTQ+ youth, for example, are inseparable unique elements of a social network made up of five different systems: microsystem, mesosystem, exosystem, macrosystem, and chronosystem. Empathizing with LGBTQ+ youth through the lens of Bronfenbrenner's ecological systems theory leads to understanding the impact surrounding systems have upon individuals.

Microsystem:
- The individual, their biology, or specific religious and cultural contexts, and unique peer groups.
- Microsystems also include home and domestic life, immediate neighbors, and classroom.

Mesosystem:
- The connection and interplay between places like home, school, and neighborhood where each individual interacts.

Exosystem:
- Local industry, the school boards, mass media, and parental workplaces that impact LGBTQ+ youth even if they don't directly access these organizations.
- Major institutions that reflect culture, practices, policies, and even legislation enacted.
- The links that can occur between a setting where one doesn't have an active role and their immediate context. For example, laws on marriage equality do not directly affect young LGBTQ+ people who may not be old enough to marry, but those laws do impact how they see themselves, their future, and their sense of belonging in a community.

Macrosystem:
- The layer of social-ecology that binds the other interacting layers together.
- The dominant set of beliefs that organize the other systems beneath it, and refers to culture, customs, countries, and socioeconomic status, as well as attitudes that shape large groups of people.

Chronosystem:
- The interplay of life transitions, environmental events, and socio-historical influences on people.
- The pattern of environmental events and changes that occur, and the socio-historical circumstances surrounding these changes.

Introduction to Part II 89

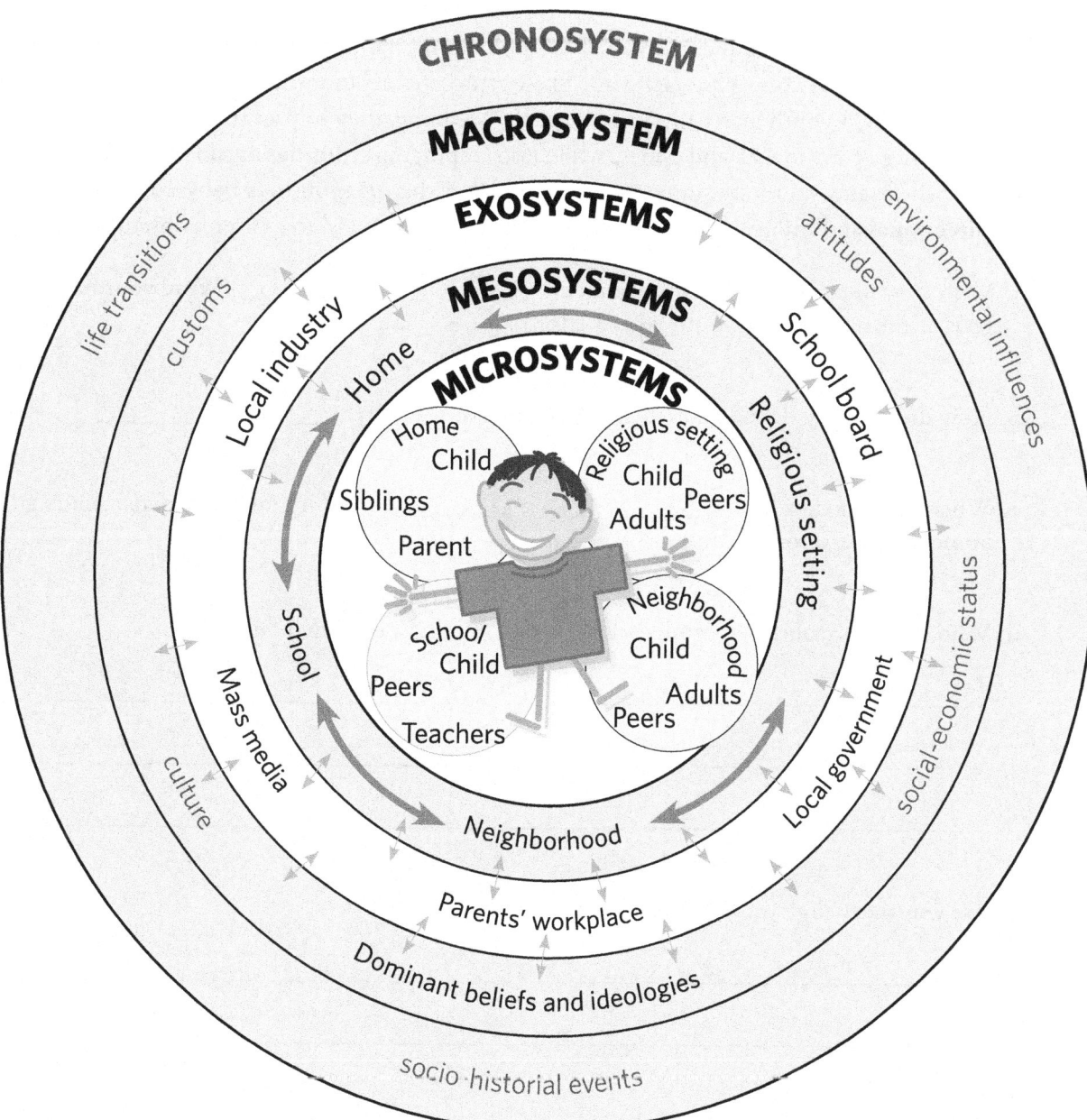

PRACTICE

The following worksheet is useful for both chapters Eight and Nine, and can be used by the clinician or educator, as well as with LGBTQ+ youth, too. It is intended to create an overview of the different systems interacting in the lives of youth.

1a. MICROSYSTEMS

Microsystems are the unique individual, school, home, family, neighborhood, or religions that LGBTQ+ youth have direct contact with. These structures, relationships, biology, and organizations impact LGBTQ+ youth internally and externally. Meaning, they impact the youth from within, like the influence of hormones and genes, while also impinging from the outside, like toxins, cultural views, beliefs, and values. It's important to remember that relationships between microsystems are **bi-directional** and influence one another in a back and forth fashion (Bronfenbrenner, 1979).

a. Who are you considering at this moment? _____ (Write your name if it's you, or the name of the youth you care for.)

b. How do you/they define your/their gender and/or sexuality? _____

c. Where do you/they live? _____ (With family, friends, alone, group home, homeless, foster care?)

d. Who is part of your/their family? (List parents, siblings, extended family.)

_____

_____

_____

e. Are you/they religious? What is your/their religion?

_____

_____

f. Who are your/their friends and acquaintances?

_____

_____

g. Which school do you/they attend?

_____

_____

h. What are your/their teachers like?

_____

_____

i. What is the neighborhood you/they live in like?

_____

_____

These nine questions help you get more clarity about the different microsystems in a person's life.

1b. MESOSYSTEM

These eight questions help you get more clarity about how the different mesosystems interact with each other in a dynamic way.

Mesosystem describes the relationships between microsystems.

a. Thinking about your/their home, how do you/they interact with it? Are you/they involved in the care and sustainability of it? If so, how? If not, why?

_____
_____

b. How are the interactions between the people who live in your/their home?

_____
_____

c. Thinking about your/their religious setting (if applicable), how are your interactions with that microsystem, the ideology, people, and rituals?

_____
_____

d. Consider the neighborhood you/they live in. What is it like?

_____
_____

e. Do you/they interact with others in your their neighborhood? How is it?

_____
_____

f. Do you/they go to any community events, services, or offerings? Are there any LGBTQ+ organizations, clubs, and places where you/they are/can be involved?

_____
_____

g. When thinking about your/their school, what is it like? Is it welcoming and inclusive? Is there a GSA? Why/why not?

_____
_____

h. How are your/their interactions with school? This is an important question to consider, so please take time to answer it, and use another piece of paper if needed.

_____
_____

1c. EXOSYSTEM

The exosystem is a larger organization of people serving the community that impacts the lives of LGBTQ+ youth, even though the youth themselves don't have any power in those exosystems. Examples of exosystems include: local government, the school board, local industry, mass media, and parental workplaces.

These six questions help you get more clarity about how the different exosystems impact LGBTQ+ youth.

a. The school board is a major influencer upon the lives of LGBTQ+ youth. From the laws they enforce to the policies they implement, top-down power systems impact LGBTQ+ youth in very specific and potentially harmful ways. Thinking about yourself (or the person you care for), how do educational laws and policies affect you/them?

_____

_____

_____

b. Although school boards have great influence upon the lives of LGBTQ+ youth, the youth themselves have little to no power to affect these exosystems. Reflect now on the experience and impact of having little power to effect change in the school board exosystems that control you, or the person you care for.

_____

_____

_____

c. The local government is intended to be a place of democratic involvement, however; only 50 to 55 percent of eligible voters turned out to vote in presidential elections in the United States in 2012 and in 2016 (Peters & Wooley, 2017; Wallace, 2016). This suggests that US citizens do not participate in government. What impact does this have on you, or the LGBTQ+ person you care about?

_____

_____

_____

d. Some organizations in the U.S. have policies that are unfriendly to LGBTQ+ people. If this is true for you, or the LGBTQ+ person you care about, please describe it below. Not all parental workplaces are discriminatory and impact LGBTQ+ youth, but it can happen.

_____

_____

_____

e. Mass media send messages everyday about what people need, how they should live their lives, who matters, and who does not. Looking at the advertising and media messages you've seen in the last 24 to 72 hours, what messages are offered about LGBTQ+ people?

_____

_____

_____

f. Local industry refers to the stores and businesses that exist in your community. Thinking about the ones you (or the LGBTQ+ person you care about) go/goes to, what messages do they offer to the LGBTQ+ community? Some may not offer any messages at all. That's also something to write about.

_____

_____

_____

1d. MACROSYSTEMS

Macrosystems are the culture and ideology that shape values, laws, policy, and standards of conduct. It influences individuals directly even if they don't influence it at all. Examples of macrosystems include democracy; capitalism; socialism; religions such as Hinduism, Islam, Christianity, and Judaism; and ethnic groups such as being Asian or Indian, for example. Macrosystems also create the conditions for intersectionality - the various social, cultural, biological, racial, religious, and ethnic identities that intersect and lead to increased rates of discrimination and oppression.

- Thinking about the various ideologies that you (or the LGBTQ+ person you care about) are/is exposed to, how do they impact you/them? Ideologies can include religions, ethnicities, and cultures.

_____

_____

_____

1e. CHRONOSYSTEM

Bronfenbrenner (1979) referred to the chronosystem as the collection of unique life experiences a person has while interacting with the various systems. It includes life transitions and the person's unique history. In the space provided below, write all about your/the other person's unique life story.

_____

_____

_____

_____

_____

_____

REFLECT

- This is the framework used for Part II, and also for understanding *Educational Trauma*.

- You can fill out the form above with any LGBTQ+ youth you care about in mind, or you can give it to them to complete about themselves. When you complete it about someone else, it's an activity that compliments Chapter Eight.

- When you offer this form to an LGBTQ+ youth you care about, it reflects the activities in Chapter Nine.

2. EDUCATIONAL TRAUMA

LEARN

Educational Trauma is the systemic and cyclical harm faced by students, educators, parents, administrators, and communities as a result of interacting educational systems (Gray, 2013, 2015, 2016). It is perpetrated inadvertently in many instances, and exists on a spectrum ranging from mild to so severe as to ruin a person's life.

The spectrum of Educational Trauma explains the pervasive trauma rampant in schools, and is a range of events impacting communities by spreading a sense of helplessness and feelings of disempowerment. Poor communities, people of color, and LGBTQ+ youth are among those most vulnerable to Educational Trauma (Snapp et al., 2015; Losen & Gillespie, 2012).

> *My teen collaborators define Educational Trauma as any trauma that happens at school.*

PRACTICE

The Spectrum of Educational Trauma

The following are examples of harm occurring in schools:

- Testing and grade-based/age-based standardized curricula
- Bullying of/by educators
- Bullying of/by students
- Collective punishment
- Corporal punishment
- Special and gifted education
- ADHD and the use of stimulant medication
- Rejection, harassment, abuse, assault, and bathroom/locker room issues related to LGBTQ+ youth in schools
- The School-to-Prison Pipeline and the legal segregation of black, brown, poor, and LGBTQ+ youth (for more, see Chapter 11, #6) (Alexander, 2012; Losen & Gillespie, 2012; Snapp et al., 2015)

Signs and Symptoms of Educational Trauma

- Resistance to school tasks and assignments
- Low self-esteem
- School refusal
- Eating disorders
- Anxiety and sadness
- Aversion to school events
- Feelings of worthlessness, hopelessness, and powerlessness
- Mood disorders
- Failure to function at average/expected levels; doesn't meet potential
- Theft
- Learning difficulties
- Low or inconsistent academic achievement
- Attention problems
- Substance abuse
- Aggressive behavior
- Disruptive behavior
- Oppositional behavior
- Defiance
- Irritability
- Explosive behavior
- Suicidal and/or homicidal ideation

Misdiagnoses of Educational Trauma:
- Generalized Anxiety Disorder
- Major Depressive Disorder
- Learning disabilities

- Disorders of communication, such as Receptive and Expressive Language Disorders and Selective Mutism

- Oppositional Defiant Disorder

- Attention Deficit Disorder/Attention Deficit Hyperactivity Disorder

- Intermittent Explosive Disorder

- Somatic problems

- Post-Traumatic Stress Disorder

- Eating disorders

REFLECT

- Thinking about the LGBTQ+ youth you care about, do any of these experiences resonate with the ones they report?

- Now, reflecting on the educational system, school policies, and the laws that govern how students learn, are there any you disagree with? Why or why not?

- Could you see yourself standing up and advocating for LGBTQ+ youth in schools where Educational Trauma happens disproportionately to them every day (Snapp et al.)?

- If and when you do voice your opposition to harmful educational practices that have been normalized in our culture, by laws and policies, you will be serving an important role!

> *One action doesn't remedy the system, yet it is critical to the system being remedied!*

Compassion, Countertransference, and Counterreaction to LGBTQ+ Youth

This chapter opens Part II with the first of two chapters on the individual level of caring for LGBTQ+ youth. This one demonstrates how clinicians and educators can practice compassion strategies and interventions (Gilbert, 2009) while caring for/educating LGBTQ+ youth. Since it's for the professional, it also addresses the countertransference/counterreactions that can arise and interfere with compassion, education, and treatment. The role and prevalence of trauma in the lives of LGBTQ+ youth is disproportionately high, inviting self-loathing, rejection, abuse, abandonment, homelessness, and suicidality.

These consequences can be mitigated with interventions that promote acceptance, commitment, and the willingness to take action to relieve suffering.

However, clinicians and educators need cognitive and emotional flexibility, which are key aspects of Acceptance and Commitment Therapy (ACT), to do so. This chapter explores and improves the biases and reactions that impede educating and treating LGBTQ+ youth.

1. **BIAS BLITZ**

LEARN

Whether we realize it or not, we all hold implicit biases. One way of managing bias is by acknowledging it and cultivating less judgment. The following questions can facilitate awareness of bias, for the purpose of releasing it.

PRACTICE

What are all the myths you hold/held/heard/believe/believed about LGBTQ+ people? List everything, including incomplete thoughts and single words. No judgment, just let it flow out.

_____
_____
_____

Could you see yourself letting go of any of the beliefs or values listed above? If not, that's ok; ask yourself why and write the answer here.

_____
_____
_____

Have you ever noticed your views affecting the treatment you offer? Would your patient feel okay hearing about some of your views? Explore the ways views/beliefs/values keep people separate and impact relationships.

_____
_____
_____

REFLECT

- Self-kindness and self-acceptance arise when we integrate the darker parts of our personality.

- When working with LGBTQ+ youth, it's important to know where your biases lie. It's one step towards identifying and integrating your shadow/dark parts.

- If you're not ready to explore your biases yet, it's ok. Many people aren't. See if you can be open to it one day.

- If you looked at your biases, and don't know what to do with them, or feel ashamed or overwhelmed, it's ok too. These are common reactions. Letting go of maladaptive patterns requires looking at them and acknowledging them first. Way to go!

- Seeking consultation is another way to overcome bias and bring even more meaningful and effective treatments and pedagogies to LGBT+ youth.

BIAS BLITZ

What are all the myths you hold/held/heard/believe/believed about LGBTQ+ people? List everything, including incomplete thoughts and single words. No judgment, just let it flow out.

_____

_____

_____

_____

Could you see yourself letting go of any of the beliefs or values listed above? If not, that's ok; ask yourself why and write the answer here.

_____

_____

_____

_____

Have you ever noticed your views affecting the treatment you offer? Would your child feel okay hearing about some of your views? Explore the ways views keep people separate and impact relationships.

_____

_____

_____

_____

*Modification:

When working with large groups of people (professionals or students), divide the group up into "families" of 8-12 people. Invite the "families" to verbally discuss the questions on this page.

This can also be used as an oral activity in families, when their LGBTQ+ youth is **not** present.

2. COUNTERTRANSFERENCE, COUNTER-REACTION, AND TRANSFERENCE

LEARN

Countertransference, counterreaction, and transference are experiences that happen in the therapeutic relationship. They mimic instances that arose in other relationships, and when processed tenderly, can be released and cleared. These three types of experiences also arise between teachers and students, parents and their kids, even between partners, friends, and lovers. Super tricky stuff to track and utilize in the moment, but it is possible!

Definitions:

Transference reactions arise in therapeutic relationships when individuals experience unconscious reactions, beliefs, feelings, attitudes, and values about/towards their clinician.

This can also happen in school settings. For example, a teacher may be on the receiving end of a transference type of reaction when a student comes out to the teacher and expects them to react as their own father or mother would. When this happens in relationships that are *not clinical or therapeutic*, the experience is called "**recapitulation**" instead of "transference." Generally, transference and recapitulation mean the same thing. The only difference is transference happens with a clinician; recapitulation can happen with anyone, anywhere, at any time.

Countertransference is a clinical term for feelings clinicians unintentionally experience when working with LGBTQ+ individuals. This phenomenon is not exclusive to LGBTQ+ individuals; however, it does carry unique significance if the clinician has unresolved relationships, issues, and problems related to their gender and/or sexuality. Countertransference can be a big problem in therapy and requires great strength, skill, courage, sensitivity, and self-kindness to be of use to both the therapist and the LGBTQ+ youth they work with. Let's just say that managing countertransference is a master clinical skill. In clinical relationships, the power of countertransference lies in how the clinician uses it to understand LGBTQ+ youth. Beginning to notice it is a kind and mindful approach to relationships of all kinds. In all relationships other than the clinical kind, these types of reactions should be treated as your own recapitulation reaction to LGBTQ+ youth.

Counterreaction is another kind of experience that can happen to clinicians, parents, educators, and other professionals, too. The difference between counterreaction and countertransference is the former is typically a reaction anyone would have to the person in question. The latter, countertransference, arises when the clinician's unresolved issues are triggered by the LGBTQ+ youth they care for. Both the teacher and the student, clinician and patient, or parent and child can unconsciously remind one another of past relationships and incidents. Without any awareness that this is happening, adults can unwittingly be reactive, instead of being responsive and reflective. Counterreactions and recapitulations happen in all relationships. Gaining mindfulness about them leads to increased empathy and compassion for LGBTQ+ youth.

(2a.) PRACTICE: EXPLORING INTERNAL BIASES

What are your internal biases? Take a deep breath and truly dig deep inside and see if there are any biases you hold. It's safe. Only you need to write, see, and/or become aware of them.

_____
_____
_____

How might you offer yourself kindness and acceptance while acknowledging you hold biases?

_____
_____
_____

How might you offer kindness and acceptance to LGBTQ+ youth who may be different/similar to you and evoke a wide range of feelings, beliefs, values, memories, desires, aversions, etc.?

_____
_____
_____

How might you find acceptance of the ever-changing nature of your thoughts and welcome new ones? Could you imagine yourself having a beginner's mind, becoming a child again, if you will, and listening to LGBTQ+ youth and the important information they share?

_____
_____
_____

Can you imagine being truly open to LGBTQ+ youth, as if they are experts beyond their years, and even beyond your experience and training? See if you can offer them this heightened level of respect and empathy; with it you grow as an adult who cares for young people.

_____
_____

REFLECT

- Don't believe everything you think.

- When you reduce the tendency to interpret thoughts, images, feelings, and memories as the grounds for reality, you also begin resisting implicit and automatic bias.

- Resisting bias is especially important when working with LGBTQ+ youth because their authentic nature is inconsistent with the dominant culture and they are subject to stereotyping, bias, and harm as a result.

- Internal and implicit biases are harmful in subtle and insidious ways. Avoiding them requires heightened awareness and sensitivity, as well as the willingness to release assumptions and entertain new ideas.

- To go even deeper, and release more bias, return to the Bias Blitz on page 104. Completing it, along with the exercise on the previous page, increases your mindful awareness about your implicit biases.

2b. PRACTICE: CLEARING COUNTERTRANSFERENCE

List all the trigger issues you have. Trigger issues are events, smells, tastes, music, sounds, tactile sensations, personality types, anniversaries, holidays, rituals, etc. that elicit a spontaneous negative reaction. They are usually unresolved issues. (For example: Sometimes people are irrationally angry in traffic; road rage can be elicited by a host of unconscious trigger issues the driver encounters.)

_____
_____
_____

Now, take a deep breath all the way down into your belly. Finding contact with your body, allow yourself to truly come into the present moment. Take as long as you need, and breathe as many times as feels right to you. Next, see if any *other trigger issues* come to mind. Give yourself time to let things rise to the surface. It's ok if nothing does.

_____
_____
_____

Are there any youth you prefer to avoid? Describe them? Why do you avoid them?

_____
_____
_____

Whom do they remind you of?

_____
_____
_____

REFLECT

- Upon completion of the questions above, allow yourself a moment to honor your courage and bravery in facing unresolved issues that may lead to countertransference.

- Your bravery and courage in this area are forms of strength in vulnerability, and cultivate mindful awareness.

- Try to practice bringing this level of mindful awareness to your LGBTQ+ youth. They need it and the deep empathy and compassion that follow.

2c. PRACTICE: DIFFERENTIATING BETWEEN COUNTERTRANSFERENCE AND COUNTERREACTIONS TO LGBTQ+ YOUTH

List times when you reacted to LGBTQ+ youth in a way that is consistent with how you would react at home, in private, and with family or friends. We all have unresolved issues; nothing to be ashamed of. Find times when your unresolved issues drove your reaction to LGBTQ+ youth.

_____

_____

_____

Explore all the times you reacted to LGBTQ+ youth in a way that others might, too. For example, some people are curious/fascinated/obsessed/disgusted/indifferent to transbodies. This range of reactions can be based in values, cultural messages, or some type of reaction that some people have to others who are different.

_____

_____

_____

Counterreactions tend to be arousing, yet less triggering and emotionally inflaming than countertransference. Have you ever had a reaction to LGBTQ+ youth where it was excessive, intense, strong, or completely flat and absent? Some people react with curiosity and/or confusion. Explore these times.

_____

_____

_____

REFLECT

- Differentiating between counterreactions and countertransference can be tricky.

- Set the intention to be on the lookout for your own reactions, and take time to analyze them.

- Seek out a clinician who specializes in clinical supervision to further explore this topic. Sometimes therapy is needed for clinicians and/or educators, and can be helpful.

2d. PRACTICE: MANAGING LGBTQ+ YOUTH TRANSFERENCE REACTIONS

Have you ever worked with LGBTQ+ youth and suddenly, they're upset/pissed off/angry/reacting strongly to/disappointed in you? Did it come as a surprise? Were you expecting it because of their history and how you know them? Why/why not?

_____

_____

_____

LGBTQ+ youth transference reactions to clinicians and/or teachers could arise at any time. If one does, see if you can pivot the angle of your perception towards LGBTQ+ youth so you see the problem through their eyes—as if you're not even part of the interaction at all. This is hard stuff; mental gymnastics, for sure! Plus, it requires a lot of self-regulation and composure to not react. Write down any thoughts that come to mind.

_____

_____

_____

LGBTQ+ youth face high amounts of abuse, discrimination, threat, intimidation, and rejection. When they begin to have intense reactions, see if you can offer them compassion. Compassion could include accepting and reassuring comments. List compassionate comments here.

_____

_____

_____

Tell LGBTQ+ youth that they can expect to have strong reactions to people at times. It's a typical reaction to being treated unfairly in the media, in school, in politics, at home, or anywhere actually. In the space below, record the thoughts you might share with LGBTQ+ youth to show them their strong reactions are understandable. Sometimes, it diffuses the power and intensity of the reaction. Feel free to share a time when you had a strong reaction—telling the LGBTQ+ youth about it may normalize and validate their experience.

_____

_____

_____

REFLECT

- Mindful awareness can be defined as balanced open awareness, with interest, curiosity, and receptiveness. Helping LGBTQ+ youth gain awareness and acceptance of their reactions inspires self-compassion.

- When LGBTQ+ youth self-reflect on their intense reactions, they begin to access their higher Self, an infinite source of wisdom.

- Self-kindness for transference reactions is an effective method of coping with anxiety and depression, both of which can be compounded by transference reactions.

3. COMBINING ACCEPTANCE, COMMITMENT, AND COMPASSION

LEARN

The impact of discrimination and harm on LGBTQ+ youth is significant. Consequences can be mitigated with practices that promote acceptance, commitment, and the willingness to take action to relieve suffering. However, clinicians and educators need cognitive and psychological flexibility, which are key aspects of Acceptance and Commitment Therapy (ACT), to do so. The following key aspects of ACT are adapted into the following questions for use in self-managing countertransference, counterreaction, unintended bias, and youth transference.

1. **Cognitive defusion**: reduce the urge to make thoughts, images, emotions, and memories the basis for reality

2. **Acceptance**: flexibly noticing thoughts while remaining open to new ones

3. **Mindful awareness**: balanced open interest and receptiveness

4. **Self-reflection**: accessing the higher self, the infinite source of wisdom within each person

5. **Values**: assessing beliefs and importance of issues to clinicians, educators, LGBTQ+ youth, and their parents

6. **Committed action**: executive functioning, combined with the willingness to take action

PRACTICE

1. What thoughts, images, memories, and emotions come to mind when you think of LGBTQ+ youth?

   _____

   _____

2. Do these thoughts, images, memories, and emotions become the basis for your judgments and interpretations? Could you be open to other ideas?

   _____

   _____

3. Mindful awareness is balanced open interest and receptiveness of whatever is happening in the moment. When you interact with LGBTQ+ youth, are you present to their views, emotions, impulses, fears, inhibitions, etc.?

   _____

   _____

4. People often think about their experiences and next statements when listening to others. A mindful approach filters out self-centered thinking and focuses the light of attention squarely on the other person. See if you can catch yourself not being present, and re-align your attention with the LGBTQ+ youth you work with. Has it happened before? It's ok! It's quite common. The act of re-aligning attention on the other person **is the practice of becoming more mindful**. Record your reactions here.

_____

_____

5. Some experts (Dabrowski, 1964; Hayes et al., 2016; Siegel, 2014) see great value in sourcing information from within. They describe the need, and the way, some people access their higher wisdom, even if it means going against the dominant culture, their religion, or family. For LGBTQ+ youth, this is already arising and can be harnessed for even greater growth and healing. How might you assist LGBTQ+ youth in cultivating and pursuing their inner wisdom?

_____

_____

6. In the space provided, explore your values and how they are different or similar to the LGBTQ+ youth you work with. How important are these issues to you? Start by rating them on a scale of 0-10, where 0 is "not at all" and 10 is "extremely."

_____

_____

7. How might you suspend your values and proceed with the values of the LGBTQ+ youth you interact with?

_____

_____

8. Committed action is a series of steps one can take to relieve suffering, promote joy, and thrive. Executive functioning is another way of looking at committed action because it delineates the actions involved in achieving an end goal. The steps in executive functioning are:

    a. Set a goal

    b. Make a plan

    c. Carry out the plan and self-monitor to see if the plan is working

    d. Adjust the plan as necessary to increase the likelihood of success

When combined with mindful awareness and loving kindness, the willingness to take action can heal and relieve suffering. On the lines on the next page, explore your committed action steps, as well as those of the LGBTQ+ youth you work with.

Clinician/Educator	**LGBTQ+ Youth**
a. What is **your** goal in serving LGBTQ+ youth?	b. What is the goal of the **LGBTQ+ youth** you care for?
c. What is **your** plan for achieving this goal?	d. What is **their** plan?
e. Identify 3 areas **you** will self-monitor while carrying out **your** plan.	f. Identify 3 areas **they** may wish to self-monitor while carrying out **their** plan.

a. _____

b. _____

c. _____

d. _____

e. _____

f. _____

REFLECT

- The eight practice steps/reflections in this practice correspond with Acceptance and Commitment Therapy principles (Hayes et al., 2016).

- When applied to LGBTQ+ youth, these eight steps create a framework within which clinicians and educators can suspend personal values, cultivate mindful awareness, and successfully act to relieve suffering.

- It's a lot to think about all in one moment, but even if you only acquire one aspect of the eight steps listed, it can soften the experience of LGBTQ+ youth and increase the likelihood of successful outcomes.

4. COMPASSION CIRCLES FOR WORKING WITH LGBTQ+ YOUTH
(GILBERT, 2009)

LEARN

In his book *The Compassionate Mind*, Paul Gilbert states that compassion evolved out of our capacity for altruistic and caring behaviors. Behaviors such as guiding, helping, protecting, and caring for others constitute compassionate action. Gilbert suggested that these behaviors can be cultivated with attention and warmth.

Gilbert declared that *compassion circles* can be intentionally cultivated with others, and with ourselves. With concern for LGBTQ+ youth, it's helpful to develop any or all of the competencies and attributes included in Gilbert's *compassion circles*. It's an important step towards minimizing judgment and implicit bias, while increasing the level of care and attention directed towards vulnerable LGBTQ+ youth.

PRACTICE

Attributes and competencies featured in Gilbert's *Compassion Circles*:

- Non-judgment
- Empathy
- Distress tolerance (of your own distress and that of the LGBTQ+ youth you care for)
- Sympathy
- Sensitivity
- Care for well-being

SKILLS:

- Attention
- Feeling
- Sensory
- Imagery
- Reasoning
- Behavior

REFLECT

- When the skills and attributes above are cultivated, *compassion circles* are in action.
- When cultivated with warmth and directed towards LGBTQ+ youth, *compassion circles* have the potential to ripple out with incredible acts of life-affirming kindness and progress towards equality.

5. SELF-COMPASSION WHEN WORKING WITH LGBTQ+ YOUTH

LEARN

Self-compassion is cultivated with four different practices (Gray, 2016):

    i. Mindful awareness

    ii. Self-kindness

    iii. Shared humanity (remembering we all suffer at some point, in some way)

    iv. The willingness to take action to relieve your own suffering

When working with LGBTQ+ youth, clinicians and educators are exposed to increased reports of distress, victimization, trauma, and suicidality in comparison to other youth populations. Self-compassion practices are important self-care tools that reduce the risk of burnout/compassion fatigue.

PRACTICE

- This is a reminder to practice meditation or mindful awareness practices for you!

- It is also a gentle reminder to be kind to yourself, but you already know that!

- And remember, when you are suffering, you are not alone. There are others suffering along, just as there were before and will be afterwards, too.

- Finally, if you need to take action to care for yourself and relieve your own suffering, please do so. It's not just helpful for you; all of humanity benefits when you care for yourself—especially the LGBTQ+ youth you care for.

REFLECT

- Some people find it easier to care for others than to do so for themselves. Does this happen to you? If so, reflect on a new concept:

> *Your offering to others is only as vast as the gifts you bestow upon yourself!*

- Being a clinician or educator of LGBTQ+ youth involves great responsibility. How might you care for yourself, be kind to yourself, and take action when necessary so that your service to LGBTQ+ youth meets their needs?

Training LGBTQ+ Youth in Self-Compassion

Unlike the previous chapter on individual level strategies, which addresses the needs and experiences of the professional, this one shows professionals how to train LGBTQ+ youth in self-compassion. Self-compassion is associated with decreased depression and anxiety, as well as increased well-being. When applied to LGBTQ+ youth, the power arises in mitigating the extreme discrimination they face.

Reducing the risk of dissociation and decompensation due to increased rates of traumatization is an important professional responsibility when caring for LGBTQ+ youth. Self-compassion strategies for LGBTQ+ youth are offered to clinicians and educators alike, in order to promote healthy forms of courage, vulnerability, bravery, and self-kindness.

1. SELF-COMPASSION FOR LGBTQ+ YOUTH

LEARN

Self-compassion arises when people cultivate four sets of skills:

   i. Mindful awareness

   ii. Self-kindness

   iii. Shared humanity

   iv. The willingness to take action to relieve suffering

Being LGBTQ+ unfortunately invites discrimination and maltreatment in some places. By embracing your authentic identity, you're already attuned mindfully to yourself. Outward expression of your sexual and gender identity is also an act of self-kindness. When you remember that others before you have also suffered as a result of being LGBTQ+, and that others after you may also suffer, you may feel less alone in difficult times. Moreover, if you're willing to take action when times are tough, you're really in the self-compassion ballpark!

PRACTICE I

Thinking about the four parts of self-compassion practices:

   i. Mindful awareness

   ii. Self-kindness

   iii. Shared humanity

   iv. The willingness to take action to relieve suffering

Mindful awareness can be cultivated through meditation and other kinds of practices that focus attention.

Self-kindness increases with a daily *loving kindness practice*. (This is also called *Metta*, and is listed in Appendix C.)

Shared humanity is remembering that others suffer too, and that you are not alone when suffering. (This is also cultivated by practicing *Metta*, which can be found in Appendix C.)

Lastly, self-compassion and compassion involve the **willingness to take action to relieve suffering**. There's a certain amount of self-worth and agency required to take action when suffering. When you are empowered to do so, you can acquire the tools for self-preservation.

PRACTICE II

Let's evaluate the degree of self-compassion you bring to yourself.

On a scale of 1-7, where 1 = Never, and 7 = Always, please rate the following statements:

1	2	3	4	5	6	7
Never			Sometimes			Always

1. I pay attention to myself, my feelings, my experiences, and needs with tenderness. _____

2. When something important to me doesn't go well, I speak kindly to myself and offer comfort. _____

3. When times are tough, I remember that other people also suffer like I do. _____

4. When I am in pain, I do healthy things to feel better. _____

5. When I feel blue, I pause and offer myself the kindness I need. _____

6. When feeling inadequate and worthless, I remember that there are other ways to look at the situation and try to find better ways of looking at mine. _____

7. I am patient and accepting of my flaws and mistakes. _____

8. In hard times, I remember to connect with my body by breathing and/or moving. _____

9. When something that matters to me goes badly, I remember that it is part of life to fail; it happens to others, too, and I try to learn something from it. _____

10. Even though it can be hard, I try to be kind to myself when I suffer and take action to heal my pain. _____

Total Score _____

Scoring Instructions:

- *Add up your score.*
- *Under 30 – Maybe cultivate some more self-compassion*
- *40-50 – Average*
- *More than 50 – A lot of self-compassion; keep it up!*

REFLECT

- The statements are all framed towards the positive. When people actively cultivate self-compassion, these are some of the ways they try to treat themselves.

- When rating the statements, some people use lower numbers if they aren't used to being kind to themselves. It's ok to be unfamiliar with self-compassionate ways of being.

- Take time to train yourself in ways that promote higher ratings on the statements. Doing so will benefit you the most!

2. SELF-COMPASSION TRAINING PROTOCOL FOR TRAUMATIZED TEENS

LEARN

Many LGBTQ+ youth face discrimination and trauma as a result of expressing their authentic identities. Suffering is a by-product of these interactions, and self-compassion is one way LGBTQ+ youth can heal themselves while coping with social inequities.

The following protocol is adapted from *Self-Compassion for Teens: 129 Activities and Practices to Cultivate Kindness* (Gray, 2016) and is intended as a guide for clinicians and educators who care for LGBTQ+ youth. The 20 points can be used in any order and are also modified to suit the LGBTQ+ youth you're caring for.

PRACTICE

Self-Compassion Training Protocol for Traumatized Teens

1. Trust and depth in relationships

- Being LGBTQ+ can involve contact with pain, suffering, and trauma. LGBTQ+ youth require additional support to heal wounds.

- This protocol begins with the relationship between LGBTQ+ youth and their therapist or teacher, because that relationship can be a bedrock to cultivating a healing self-compassion practice.

- The therapist or educator must have a consistent self-compassion practice themselves, in order to be most helpful to LGBTQ+ youth beginning to cultivate one.

- When rapport between LGBTQ+ youth and their therapist or teacher isn't solid, it could further injure LGBTQ+ youth who've experienced trauma.

- To deepen trust and rapport, therapists and teachers are encouraged to be more available to LGBTQ+ youth.

- LGBTQ+ youth who have been through traumatic situations need clinicians and educators upon whom they can rely for support.

2. Centering and Grounding

- Centering and grounding practices (such as the one in Chapter One, #1) are effective in helping LGBTQ+ youth gain the balance, skillfulness, and resilience needed to explore pain and suffering.

- Emotional and spiritual grounding keeps LGBTQ+ youth firmly connected to the Earth, so that emotions, ideas, beliefs, and even external influences don't knock them over.

- Music can also be used to anchor LGBTQ+ youth in the present moment (Germer, 2009) and can re-orient them to something soothing and enjoyable.

- Gazing upon a tree, beloved pet, or fire are also good ways to anchor attention and center again.

- The more frequently these practices are utilized, the more effective they become.

3. Deep Body Breathing

- Guide LGBTQ+ youth to breathe deeply into their belly three times.

- Direct them to hold the in-breath for a count of five.

- Then, exhale slowly and purposefully through the mouth.

- On the out-breath, imagine pain, suffering, and negative energy, ideas, beliefs, and memories flowing out and away.

4. Build Positive and Negative Affect Tolerance

- LGBTQ+ youth who have been traumatized may have difficulty tolerating negative affect and believing that positive affect is real, possible, and safe to experience.

- To counteract this problem, LGBTQ+ youth benefit from new opportunities to increase affect tolerance in both directions.

- For negative affect, begin by scaffolding to serve as a source of support to LGBTQ+ youth, when they need it.

- To increase positive affect tolerance, invite LGBTQ+ youth to share or write down any positive feelings they experience. This can be an ongoing journal activity, for one week only, or a verbal report.

5. Define and Explore Abreaction

- Shapiro (2001) described abreaction as "the re-experiencing of the stimulated memory at a high level of disturbance."

- Abreaction can arise at any time, in response a trigger event associated with a traumatic memory.

- Abreaction is a serious event, which can involve a great deal of terror for traumatized LGBTQ+ youth.

- Explain to LGBTQ+ youth that self-compassion practices involve touching pain and suffering, which can lead to intense levels of disturbance.

- Preparing LGBTQ+ youth for possible abreaction, and creating a plan for how to cope with it, when and if it occurs, is helpful when cultivating a sustainable self-compassion practice.

6. **Establish Expectations—Feelings Are Real, but not True, and Should Be Treated as Re-Experiencing Rather Than Experiencing for Real**

    - Rinpoche & Swanson (2012) suggest that feelings are real, but they are not true. Feelings can be strong and felt as if they are completely real, in the here and now, but this isn't always so.

    - Take fear for example; when truly in danger, people rarely feel any fear at all, because they are mobilized to protect themselves from danger. When we feel fear, it is a real feeling, but it isn't necessarily true that we are in danger and need to be afraid.

    - LGBTQ+ youth need to know this about their feelings, in order to increase emotional toleration and cultivate self-compassion in the face of difficult moments.

7. **Allow Emotions to Flow Out for Complete Release**

    - Crying can be reframed as a cleansing process, and feeling feelings can move them through for clearing and release.

    - Having an emotion is one way of letting go, which is a healthy and restorative aspect of healing.

    - When a cut heals in the skin, a scab forms. Over time, the scab sloughs off. Sometimes, a new scab emerges, at other times, the wound is open for a while and then heals. Emotions are like the scab forming and falling off.

    - Permission to feel emotions, and appreciation of their purpose in the healing process, gives meaning to suffering, which also eases it.

8. **Breathe Through and With Pain**

    - Breathing deeply into and through painful moments is a very real and instant way of calming the nervous system.

    - Breathe, and focus on the sensations of breath, at any moment in order to center and ground.

    - This is effective for physical, mental, emotional, and spiritual pain.

    - The more often LGBTQ+ youth make contact with their breath, the more effective it will become in grounding and centering.

9. **Sustain Healthy Practices, Especially Around Setting Boundaries and Eliminating Toxic Situations, People, Chemicals, Foods, and Beverages**

    - Invite LGBTQ+ youth to make a commitment, and set daily intentions, to live healthfully in every way.

10. **Embrace Inner Wisdom and Intuition as a Guide**

    - Encourage LGBTQ+ youth to tune inward and see if they can hear/feel/see/know the wise part of them that holds the wisdom of the universe.

- As LGBTQ+ youth age, traumatic learning experiences, coupled with heavy emphasis on the provable, dims access and interest in intuition.

- For LGBTQ+ youth, it is crucial to healthy identity formation that they find and nurture any kind of inner wisdom that they can begin to trust. This process cultivates deep self-empathy and highly effective self-compassion.

- Finding and growing intuition is a very powerful antidote to the harmful effects of discrimination on LGBTQ+ youth.

- Being hurt leaves memories and internalized negative beliefs that further damage the self-concept of LGBTQ+ youth. To counterbalance these negative effects, inner wisdom becomes a trusted friend who is always there.

- It takes a long time to nurture this, and it is well worth the investment of time and sustained practice to do.

11. **Graciously Identify and Receive Gifts**

    - LGBTQ+ youth who have been discriminated against and traumatized can easily fall into depression. To counteract this propensity, a self-compassionate practice includes finding all the gifts that come by LGBTQ+ youth.

    - A gift can be a cancelled class, a great parking spot, or time with a good friend. It need not be a material item.

    - The more LGBTQ+ youth train themselves to notice "gifts," more "gifts" will appear. It's the law of attraction coupled with the perceptual tendencies to find what we seek.

    - Graciously receiving gifts is an important part of increasing the flow of gifts. This includes being grateful, not only with the words "thank you," but also deep within the heart.

12. **Actively Reduce Stress and Increase Joyful Activities**

    - Help LGBTQ+ youth learn to avoid activities and people that cause stress.

    - Promote discovery of activities, people, places, and things that bring joy.

    - It is self-compassionate to act to relive suffering. One way of doing so is by reducing stress, and increasing pleasure.

    - Healing happens when LGBTQ+ youth rest, play, find joy, and live in alignment with their true nature.

13. **Request and Receive Help When Needed**

    - Like identifying and graciously receiving gifts, requesting and receiving help is another aspect of self-compassion practice.

- Trauma can create trust issues, which prevent LGBTQ+ youth from requesting and accepting help.

- Please remind LGBTQ+ youth that requesting and receiving assistance when needed is an act of self-compassion; one to be taken as often as needed in order to heal.

- Help LGBTQ+ youth see that some people are trustworthy and helpful, while others may not be. As they begin requesting help, they will learn more about whom they can and cannot trust. This cycle of trying and failing, learning, and trying again repeats itself throughout the lifespan.

14. **Welcome Trustworthy People Into Your Life**

    - This can be as easy as setting a daily intention to welcome trustworthy people.

    - The more LGBTQ+ youth fix their attention on welcoming trustworthy people in their lives, the more trustworthy people will show up.

    - Set limits and boundaries with toxic people, substances, and activities, too.

15. **Practice Loving Kindness for Mind, Body, Emotions, Soul, Other People, the Environment, Animals, and All Beings Everywhere**

    - The loving kindness practice (Appendix C) is a main component of cultivating self-compassion. It is also very helpful when LGBTQ+ youth heal trauma.

    - *Metta* is a direct route to retraining attention and brain connections with kindness becoming the predominant way of being.

    - Encourage LGBTQ+ youth to extend their loving kindness practice to their mind, body, soul, other people (as is typical in the practice) as well as animals, and all beings everywhere.

    - This kind of practice softens one's approach to life and promotes healing from trauma.

    - It also creates a loving kindness mindset, which lends warmth and tenderness to every interaction and action.

16. **Have Fun!**

    - Our true nature is the state of joy, and yet we aren't able to have it 100 percent of the time.

    - The juxtaposition of joy and pain creates the capacity for pleasure.

    - Fun times and activities are a great way to return to that natural state of being after trauma.

    - It is not easy to pursue fun when traumatized; however, this point in the protocol is meant to remind and emphasize the importance of fun in healing and recovering from trauma.

    - Any kind of play and enjoyment is encouraged and recommended with the same priority and importance as school, medication, or any other intervention.

17. **Positive Reality: Focus on What You Want**

    - This is a reminder to LGBTQ+ youth to let go of any thoughts, ideas, and beliefs that do not serve their highest good.

    - This goes beyond kind self-talk to the release of any and all stories that are not in alignment with the highest good of LGBTQ+ youth.

    - Help LGBTQ+ youth learn to use language that frames ideas in the positive and speaks to what they truly want. Assist in finding whatever it is that their heart longs for; let that be the focus of their communication.

    - This is a gentle way of re-directing negative self-talk or beliefs to a more self-compassionate place.

18. **Honoring Unique Needs and Talents**

    - Although we know we are all unique, there are so many ways we are clumped together and expected to behave the same.

    - A self-compassionate approach to the unique needs of LGBTQ+ youth involves gently reminding them that honoring their uniqueness is worthwhile.

    - This is ever more important when recovering from trauma because uniqueness can be internalized as damaged, disgusting, unlovable, and worse.

19. **Have Open and Honest Communication With Respect for All Life**

    - Encourage LGBTQ+ youth to speak openly and honestly with those they trust.

    - Invite them to be as honest as they can with themselves.

    - It takes courage and bravery to open to the truth in any moment.

    - Remind LGBTQ+ youth how very strong they truly are.

20. **Allow Things to Be in Their Own Time, Starting With Yourself**

    - Healing trauma takes a long time.

    - Healing takes patience.

    - It takes effort and a lot of energy.

    - The more time and energy that are applied to healing, the more effective it is.

- Each one of us is endowed with self-healing properties; our bodies know exactly how to heal cuts and wounds. We also have everything within us to heal mental, emotional, and spiritual wounds.

- Facilitate LGBTQ+ youth having the time and space they needs to feel safe and to heal wounds.

REFLECT

- The components of the protocol may not be comfortable for everyone.

- Use the elements that feel right, modify those that can be, and discard those that do not resonate.

- For traumatized LGBTQ+ youth, it is important to start self-compassion training with this protocol. The protocol is sufficient for initiating a self-compassion practice, and need not be expanded upon until such time as LGBTQ+ youth decide to.

3. SCAFFOLDING LGBTQ+ YOUTH FOR SELF-ADVOCACY & EMERGING ADULT INTERDEPENDENCE

LEARN

How might LGBTQ+ youth learn to advocate for themselves and pursue interdependence in relationships? This question blends three different developmental challenges for LGBTQ+ youth into one!

    a. Gender and sexual identity development

    b. Self-advocacy

    c. Interdependence

The first challenge, gender identity development is addressed in detail in Chapter Five, while sexual identity is addressed is Chapter One. The practice below covers all three domains in two steps as LGBTQ+ youth develop into adulthood.

PRACTICE

Silently say to yourself:

> "What do I need to be happy and thrive?"

Now, pause for a quiet moment, and see what arises…

When you know what you need, you can tell others. Use the following template and fill in the blanks to fit different situations:

I observe _____.

I feel _____.

I need _____.

I request _____.

REFLECT

- It can be challenging to identify needs and articulate them to other people.

- What is it like for you to rely on other people to meet your needs?

- What is it like to find the words for your needs? If it's a challenge, look up Marshall Rosenberg's list of universal human needs in *Non-Violent Communication*.

Safety Issues, Acceptance, and Outcomes

This chapter takes a look at what clinicians and educators can do to support the families of LGBTQ+ youth. It includes offering safety for parental reactions of grief, loss, disappointment, resistance, fear, aversion, worry, and sparing youth from these reactions. Engaging activities are offered to help clinicians and educators assess and explore the family's readiness to support LGBTQ+ youth. The importance of parental support in long-term outcomes for LGBTQ+ youth frames the practices, activities, and worksheets contained in this chapter.

1. PARENTAL ACCEPTANCE AND SUPPORT

LEARN

Family acceptance of LGBTQ+ youth has been demonstrated as the greatest protective factor against negative physical and mental health outcomes (Ryan et al., 2009). Researchers found that high family rejection is associated with LGB, and some T, youth being:

- 8.4x more likely to have attempted suicide
- 5.9x more likely to report high levels of depression
- 3.4x more likely to use illegal drugs
- 3.4x more likely to be at high risk for HIV and STDs

> *Latino males retrospectively reported experiencing the highest levels of rejection for their sexual orientation during the teen years.*

It's important to confront families with this information and data. (Several pages of facts and statistics are included in Appendix B for you to give to parents.) For one, this kind of information prompts parents to think about how impactful they can be. We're talking about suicide attempts, depression, substance abuse, and high-risk sexual activity as a result of parental reaction and beliefs. For parents who are supporting their LGBT youth as best they can, this information may serve as validation and a reminder that being there for LGBTQ+ youth is critical to their survival and long-term health.

PRACTICE

Parental reactions can run the gamut. There are many different kinds of reactions parents have when they learn their kids are LGBTQ+. Feelings of all sorts are okay and common, even if they are difficult, uncomfortable, and unsettling. Explore the following list, and see which feelings you've encountered as a parent, since learning your child is LGBTQ+.

- Surprise
- Shock
- Grief
- Loss
- Disappointment
- Fear
- Worry
- Concern
- Joy
- Celebration
- Affirmation
- Confirmation
- Neutrality
- Indifference

- Acceptance
- Love
- Affinity
- Closeness
- Intimacy
- Distance
- Anger
- Confusion
- Validation

All feelings are okay, though not all reactions are. It is important that you keep certain negative feelings to yourself, and not react with anger, aggression, rage, and threats. Clinicians and educators have the responsibility of shielding LGBTQ+ youth from these kinds of reactions, *and* giving you a safe space to express this—separate and apart from your kids.

REFLECT

- As parents, clinicians, and educators, exploring difficult feelings between parents and their youth can be challenging. Some people and professionals have a hard time with differences and strong negative feelings. Trust that taking the time to look within at these reactions literally strengthens all parties.

2. ASSESS RISKS OF COMING OUT TO FAMILY

LEARN

When LGBTQ+ youth come out to clinicians and educators, it doesn't always mean they've also come out to their parents, friends, or other family members. In other cases, friends and family may learn before educators, counselors, and parents.

> *Be sensitive and inquire about whom else your LGBT+ youth may have come out to.*
>
> *Do not make any assumptions; unintentionally outing someone can have disastrous consequences.*

Use the following questionnaire, **with youth**, to assess any risks that may arise when LGBTQ+ youth come out.

REFLECT

- Discuss the answers to assessing risk.

- Create concrete plans and take action to report any threats of violence, homicide, and suicide, when and wherever necessary.

- Seek intensive treatment for any substance abuse problems and/or self-harm activities.

- Be mindful and attentive to the needs of LGBTQ+ youth, and be willing to act as an advocate on their behalf.

ASSESSING RISK QUESTIONNAIRE

1. What do you think will happen when you tell _____ you are _____?

2. What is *your* opinion of your parents'/family's/friends'/community's openness to the LGBTQ+ community?

3. What are *their* views and values?

4. What are some comments and values about your culture and family around differences, diversity, non-conforming gender expression, and sexuality?

5. Is there anyone you trust more when considering coming out? Is there anyone who may be most receptive and supportive?

6. When you share with someone other than parents, is there any risk your parents will still find out?

7. Is there anyone in your family you may not yet be ready to come out to? Why?

8. Create safety plans around potentially dangerous scenarios (i.e., collect resources and find the local LGBTQ+ youth center, friends, or extended family members who can help in an emergency).

9. How can you take care of yourself?

10. How might you offer yourself kindness, self-compassion, and the tenderness you need when coming out?

3. ASSESSING RELIGIOUS BELIEFS

LEARN

Religion plays a very large role in some families and cultures. While it may be waning in some parts of the country, it's thriving in others. LGBTQ+ youth who come from religious families face an extra hurdle when embracing and affirming their authentic identity.

The following questions tease out some of the errors of logic and fact that get wrapped into religion.

PRACTICE

1. What religion/ethnicity/culture does this family affiliate with?

2. Explore the perfection of divine will, even in situations that are difficult.

3. Ask parents to explain their religion's view of martyrs. It opens the door to touch on historical examples where something "was meant to be," even if people didn't like it or expect it.

4. When transpeople begin taking hormones, transition, and have surgeries, many experience relief of symptoms that previously could have led to suicide. The presence of such great relief for transpeople is miraculous, and can be viewed as divine inspiration of humankind in solving life's challenges.

5. Sacrament is the external expression of grace. When LGBTQ+ youth authentically express themselves, it's an example of the sacred.

6. Many religions have LGBTQ+ groups. This reflects an evolution in humanity and spirituality. Many evolutions have arisen since the Old and New Testament, as well as the *Koran* and other religious texts. Evolution has left some religious practices, such as keeping concubines, and sacrificing animals and people, obsolete.

7. Historically and culturally there are many examples of LGBTQ+ people succeeding and being happy. The Fa'afaine in Somalia are one example of a culture accepting third gender people. Take time to educate parents about these examples so they can see how other cultures accept it as a natural variation of humanity.

REFLECT

- Religion and culture tend to be rigid. Respect the views of others and remember the goal here is not to change any view, but rather challenge and assess thinking patterns.

- See if there is any mental flexibility that could allow parents to embrace both their LGBTQ+ youth and their religion. Wisdom is the ability to simultaneously hold contradictory ideas.

- Sometimes planting seeds of new and different ideas is the only thing to do. The rest comes later; often without your involvement or knowledge.

4. LGBTQ+ FAMILY FIESTA

LEARN

This activity builds on the Bias Blitz on page 104; however, it is modified for use with families. Provide each member of the family who is present for treatment a copy of the Family Fiesta worksheet on the next page. This activity is intended for youth and families who are further along in the coming out process. **Do not do it with LGBTQ+ youth present, if the family is early in the coming out process.**

PRACTICE

Give each member of the family present a copy of the Family Fiesta sheet on the next page. Allow 15-20 minutes for them to discuss and research the internet to find definitions of terms on the list.

Could you see yourself letting go of any of the beliefs or values listed above? If not, that's ok; ask yourself why and write the answer here.

_____

_____

_____

_____

Have you ever noticed your views affecting your relationships? Would your LGBTQ+ child feel okay hearing some of your views? Explore beliefs that can keep people separate and negatively impact relationships.

_____

_____

_____

_____

REFLECT

Families taking the time to learn about terms and definitions related to the LGBTQ+ community creates closeness as well as informed and mindful family members. May the ensuing discussion be an enlightening fiesta for all!

LGBTQ+ FAMILY FIESTA

Provide each member of the family who is present with their own copy of this sheet. This activity is intended for youth and families who are further along in the coming out process.

Define the following terms:

- Gay _____
- Lesbian _____
- Bisexual _____
- Polysexual _____
- Pansexual _____
- Omnisexual _____
- Skoliosexual _____
- Demisexual _____
- Grey Ace _____
- Asexual _____
- Polyamory _____
- Intersex _____
- Transfemale _____
- Transmale _____
- Cisgender _____
- Transgender _____
- Agender _____
- Genderfluid _____
- Genderqueer _____
- Bigender _____

- Trigender _____
- Two-spirit _____
- Third/Fourth/Fifth gender _____
- Pangender _____
- Demigirl _____
- Demiboy _____
- Ladyboy _____
- Androgyne _____
- Intergender _____
- Nonbinary _____
- Questioning _____
- Homoromantic _____
- Bromantic _____
- Panromantic _____
- Aromantic _____

*Modification:

This activity can be conducted as a family discussion. Providing each member with this page offers a visual prompt to follow along with, and take notes if desired.

5. FAMILIES COME OUT, TOO

LEARN

Parents, siblings, aunts, uncles, and cousins come out, too—though in very different ways and times. The following worksheet is intended for parents who are getting used to their child's sexual orientation or gender expression, and trying to express it to others. The process of finding the words to say about what the child's, parents', siblings', and the whole family's experience is like is also part of coming out.

PRACTICE

- Apply kindness to families and their members who come out. Use the Parent Survey handout to ease parental experiences of coming out.

REFLECT

- Is there a difference between discussing coming out with family members as compared to people outside the family? There's no right or wrong answer, though it is helpful to be mindful of the differences.

- Remember nothing lasts forever, so any discomfort now will likely change somehow over time.

PARENT SURVEY

On a scale of 1-10, where 1 = not at all and 10 = completely

How comfortable are you with **your child's** sexual orientation and/or gender expression?

1   2   3   4   5   6   7   8   9   10

←--→

How comfortable are you sharing your child's sexual orientation and/or gender expression **with other people in your family**?

1   2   3   4   5   6   7   8   9   10

←--→

How comfortable are you sharing your child's sexual orientation and/or gender expression **with people outside your family**?

1   2   3   4   5   6   7   8   9   10

←--→

What might you need to increase your comfort level, if desired? Describe your needs here:

_____

_____

_____

Sometimes, it helps people to discuss coming out by first creating a sample script. Just writing out the things you might say gives you a chance to see it on paper and adjust it if necessary. Write out some preliminary thoughts, and be prepared to edit them.

_____

_____

_____

6. COMING OUT AS THE FAMILY OF TRANSYOUTH

LEARN

For transyouth, **early coming out** leads to more time in life as their authentic self. From a developmental perspective, that means less trauma and dysphoria associated with feeling like they were born in the wrong body or assigned the wrong gender. Early coming out for transyouth can mean avoiding later surgeries, avoiding problematic symptoms, increased social acceptance, and also increased likelihood of a typical gender experience. In low acceptance communities and families, early coming out can be a very risky event possibly leading to homelessness, as well as physical and emotional abuse.

Consider this paradox:

Family rejection -> really bad

Family acceptance -> really good

Family reaction is an influential variable

PRACTICE

Since early coming out is associated with better outcomes, parents who are open to it can facilitate healthy development. Share the following with parents of transyouth—they need to know this:

Coming out for transyouth can occur multiple times, even with parents:

1. **Telling parents:** It's challenging to tell parents, and in some cases, parents already know.

2. **Accessing medical treatment** (i.e., puberty blockers, hormones, surgery): In accessing medical care of any kind, but especially transition related care, transyouth need to disclose their gender.

3. **Name change:** When transyouth change their name, they essentially come out to everyone they know and ask them to use a different name.

4. **Use of preferred pronouns:** While many transyouth feel their expressed gender from a young age, it's new for their families and they easily slip into old habits, names, and pronouns. Transyouth face having to correct their parents and family members when dead names and other gender pronouns are used, creating 'coming out' instances over and over again.

5. **Physical effects of taking hormones:** When the effects of treatment begin to show, it can lead transyouth to come out because non-binary gender expression (or gender assigned at birth) becomes too difficult to uphold any longer.

Coming out can lead to:

- Violence

- Homelessness

- Rejection

It's a very real concern for many transyouth!

Facilitate transyouth coming out by being sensitive to these changes in their lives.

REFLECT

- Discuss these risks of coming out with parents, and assess if any exist for the transyouth you work with.

- Empower parents to support transyouth coming out when and how they are ready to.

- Offer parental support for the challenges they face with their child's transition. All feelings are expected, and ok.

Making School Safe for LGBTQ+ Youth

School is a place where young people expect to find safety and sanctuary; however, LGBTQ+ youth frequently run into serious problems. The problems are highlighted in the 2015 (GLSEN collected new data on school climate in 2017, and an update will be available in Fall 2018). Gay Lesbian and Straight Education Network (GLSEN) National School Climate Survey, which documented LGBTQ+ youth are truant more often because of hostile school climates. 32% of LGBTQ+ students surveyed by GLSEN "did not plan to finish high school, or were not sure if they would finish, indicated that they were considering dropping out because of the hostile climate created by gendered policies and practices" (2015). Moreover, hostile school climates lead to poorer psychological health, including increased rates of depression, lower self-esteem, and a sense of not belonging.

With all of these school-based concerns, how might clinicians and educators contribute positively? The following chapter offers strategies to combat cyberbullying of LGBTQ+ youth and specific ways of engaging community members on behalf of LGBTQ+ youth, as well as methods for promoting inclusion, safety, and decency in schools. Templates of form letters are also included so professionals have a language base to address discrimination and hostility against LGBTQ+ youth in schools. Discover the multi-layered community influences feeding the mental health problems of LGBTQ+ youth, and how to address them systemically. Find ways of inviting other professionals to be advocates in dismantling the school-to-prison pipeline, and create safer, more inclusive, and affirming educational settings.

1. SOCIAL JUSTICE IN SCHOOLS

LEARN

According to Abreu et al. (2016), school counselors have an ethical responsibility to be social justice advocates for oppressed groups of students. They cite the American School Counselors Association's (ASCA) ethical standards as evidence for this point. Although this particular study is focused on school counselors, the moral responsibility extends to all adult caregivers of oppressed LGBTQ+ youth.

At the time of writing, LGBTQ+ youth are an oppressed group.

- Nine states have laws banning schools from discussing and serving the needs of sexual and gender minorities, including: Alabama, Arizona, Louisiana, Minnesota, Mississippi, Oklahoma, South Carolina, Texas, and Utah.

- In Texas, schools are mandated to "teach that homosexuality is an unacceptable 'lifestyle' and a criminal offense" (Abreu et al., 2016).

Some states are downright hostile for LGBTQ+ youth, and schools are even worse! How might clinicians, educators, and well-intended adult caregivers contribute to the well-being of LGBTQ+ youth at the community level? How might we become social justice advocates when already overloaded? You can do it; here's how!

PRACTICE

The following seven social justice strategies are adapted from Singh et al. (2010) in Abreu et al. (2016). They inspire community engagement for the betterment of LGBTQ+ students:

1. **Be politically informed**: Read and keep up on current events that pertain to LGBTQ+ individuals. Seek to learn about the laws in your state.

2. **Share information and enlighten others**: It's good to be informed; however, sharing what you know with just one other person helps promote greater sensitivity, empathy, and inclusion.

3. **Start the hard conversations**: Be brave and open the dialogue about injustices arising for LGBTQ+ youth. Have the courage to talk about sex, sexuality, bodies, and gender—starting with yourself!

4. **Be intentional in nurturing relationships**: As you interact other people, be aware of their humanity and the fragility of life. Bring extra kindness to yourself and others so that relationships thrive with love and respect.

5. **Promote student self-advocacy**: Using scaffolding, mentoring, coaching, role modeling, and/or any other method of sharing that works for you; help students learn to stand up for themselves. (The first half of this book is essentially all about how to do this and what to say!)

6. **Network with mindful data, social media, and tech strategies**: As you cultivate new connections personally and professionally, do so with mindful awareness and application

of technology, social media, and data. This level of mindfulness can also be seen as critical thinking. Think critically about the data, technology, and social media you use when exploring/discussing LGBTQ+ issues.

7. **Educate others about how to be an ally/advocate:** Just like strategy #2 encourages you to share what you know, #7 suggests you help others become allies and advocates like you.

REFLECT

- It's really important to remember that LGBTQ+ youth are subjected to greater levels of bullying, harassment, and assault than other oppressed groups. For this reason, safe spaces and GSAs need to be implemented specifically for and with LGBTQ+ youth. It is *inadequate* for safe spaces to exist for *all minority and oppressed groups*, because it diffuses the intensity and impact of harm directed to LGBTQ+ youth. They get lost in the mix, staff commonly fail to intervene because LGBTQ+ discrimination is not specifically outlined in school bullying policies.

- Social justice activism isn't for everyone. Many people shy away from it out of fear or overwhelm. In reality, education and LGBTQ+ youth concerns are civil rights issues of our times, with moral and ethical urgency. Protecting and caring for young people is part of the role of adult caregivers, with securing human rights being one aspect of that role; therefore, professionals have a moral and ethical responsibility to act.

- Social justice activism can lead to burn out/compassion fatigue. Using self-compassion practices while being an advocate creates the resilience needed for this work.

2. CHECKLIST OF ISSUES FOR SCHOOL ADVOCACY

LEARN

There's a lot to think about when advocating for change in a school. Here's a checklist of issues to consider, evaluate, and advocate for in schools and community organizations.

PRACTICE

- ☐ Is there a specific LGBTQ+ anti-bullying policy with consequences delineated?

- ☐ Does a GSA exist? If it does, it is important to know that these spaces are not enough to ensure the well-being and inclusion of LGBTQ+ youth.

- ☐ If there is a GSA on campus, find out how the LGBTQ+ youth on campus feel about it. It's important that they feel safe and welcome, and that it doesn't become a space for allies only.

- ☐ School-wide programming has been shown to alleviate discrimination, while increasing tolerance, respect, and kindness (Abreu et al., 2016). Consider planning events quarterly to create an inclusive climate.

- ☐ Are there safe spaces where LGBTQ+ youth know they can speak and interact freely? Visible social support (i.e., rainbow, ally, or safe space stickers) is required; the intention to be available and listen is insufficient.

- ☐ Collect and distribute Safe Zone stickers to colleagues, educators, administrators, and counselors at schools and community organizations so LGBTQ+ youth know who the allies are.

- ☐ Identify and dismantle anti-LGBT politics and policies in places that serve LGBTQ+ youth.

- ☐ Suggest and implement LGBTQ+ anti-bullying policies in schools.

- ☐ In-service training (professional development) for school staff increases visibility of allies and gives advocates tools to communicate to LGBTQ+ youth that they are valued members of the community.

- ☐ Please see abundant resources on the Gay Lesbian and Straight Education Network (GLSEN) and Gender Spectrum websites.

REFLECT

- What can/have you done to promote school safety and inclusion for LGBTQ+ youth?

- Are there any barriers keeping you from advocating for LGBTQ+ youth? How might you overcome these barriers and serve LGBTQ+ youth?

3. SCHOOL-WIDE STRATEGIES TO REDUCE LGBTQ+ CYBERBULLYING

LEARN

As more schools recognize the critical needs of LGBTQ+ youth, the data suggests that GSAs are important to their well-being, but inadequate in isolation (Abreu et al., 2016). One solution is to use strategies devised by Abreu et al., which incorporate diverse literature on bullying with the needs and uniqueness of LGBTQ+ youth. The following six strategies reflect the ethical responsibilities of school counselors as set forth by ACA (2014) and ASCA (2011, 2014).

PRACTICE

1. Request an update of anti-bullying policies to specifically address LGBTQ+ youth.

   - Include definitions of sexual minority and gender expansive bullying.
   - Who needs to report LGBTQ+ youth bullying, when, and how.
   - State the consequences for violating the policy.

2. Advocate for the inclusion of LGBTQ+ friendly curricula.

   - Including direct teaching on what LGBTQ+ bullying is.
   - Bring LGBTQ+ historical figures into the classroom to teach about the history and politics of the US from a diverse and inclusive perspective. Emphasize how this is not only social emotional training in empathy, but also an example of increasing critical thinking, too.

3. Design school-wide lesson plans that address LGBTQ+ bullying. Request one day per quarter be designated for learning about social justice issues, and that LGBTQ+ concerns be included in the programming.

4. Develop an LGBTQ+ taskforce to assess the LGBTQ+ anti-bullying policy and climate, as well as protections for sexual minority and gender expansive youth. The task force shall include:

   - A school counselor
   - Administrator
   - A teacher from every subject area
   - Parents
   - Community partners
   - Students

5. Nurture relationships with LGBTQ+ organizations in the community. Welcome guest speakers and workshops to educate youth in schools about heterosexism and examples of bullying and oppressive language.

6. Create a plan for how LGBTQ+ bullying will be reported by students and staff, as well as how it will be documented.

REFLECT

- These six strategies create a comprehensive approach to minimizing harm to LGBTQ+ youth in schools.

- It's ok if they don't all get implemented at once; change is hard. Trying to promote a culture of acceptance in schools takes a lot of little steps, so don't hesitate to take one step, then another, and another!

4. FORM LETTERS: LGBTQ+ YOUTH BULLIED, MISTREATED, AND/OR HAVING BATHROOM/LOCKER ROOM ISSUES

LEARN

When bullying and/or bathroom/locker room issues arise, it can be challenging to navigate for the first time. Wanting to help and having the words to do so don't always happen at the same time. The following two form letters are templates you can use to alert parents, administrators, teachers, counselors, and other staff that LGBTQ+ youth need their help.

BULLYING AND HARASSMENT

To Whom It May Concern:

The current climate in _____ (student's name)'s school is no longer tenable. She/He/Zhe/Zher/They is/are subjected to:

_____

_____

(Describe recent incidents with frequency of occurrence and dates.)

The following requests/suggestions are presented for your kind consideration:

_____

_____

(Describe possible solutions or requests for meeting to develop solutions jointly.)

Thank you for your continued commitment to _____ (student's name.) _____ (She/He or preferred pronoun) is fortunate to have you in their corner!

_____

(your name)

BATHROOMS AND LOCKER ROOMS

To Whom It May Concern:

This letter comes to you today because of our joint investment in _____ (student's name)'s well-being. _____ (Her/His or preferred pronoun) experiences in the _____ (bathroom/locker room) are unbearable and causing enormous distress. _____ (She/He or preferred pronoun) is subjected to

_____

_____

(Describe recent incidents with frequency of occurrence and dates.)

The following requests/suggestions are presented for your kind consideration:

_____

_____

(Describe possible solutions; i.e., a curtained area for any student desiring privacy, or requests for meeting to develop solutions jointly.)

Thank you for your continued commitment to _____ (student's name.) _____ (She/He or preferred pronoun) is fortunate to have your support!

Kindly,

_____
(your name)

REFLECT

- In both of these two form letters, it is important to be as explicit as possible.

- Even if the topic makes you feel uncomfortable, sex, gender, and sexuality are part of the human experience and deserve to be spoken about openly and respectfully. (Turn to Chapter Eight for more on how this topic makes you feel.)

- By writing and sending letters like the previous examples, you demonstrate courage in the face of vulnerability, which is needed for allies and advocates of LGBTQ+ youth.

5. HOW TO SPEAK WITH AND TRAIN YOUTH AND OTHER PROFESSIONALS IN BEING KIND TO LGBTQ+ YOUTH

LEARN

There are a few aspects of working with LGBTQ+ youth that differ from those of all other youth. The kindest approach involves sensitivity and empathy for these unique aspects rather than avoiding them altogether. Avoidance is a defense mechanism people use when they are uncomfortable or uncertain about a situation/feeling. Some professionals use avoidance, too, when they don't know how to respond to a given predicament.

PRACTICE

Here are a few areas to remember when cultivating kindness towards LGBTQ+ youth:

- **Pronouns matter:** Inquire about which pronouns are preferred by sharing your preferred pronouns. Do so discretely to avoid unintentionally outing. Try to avoid making assumptions about gender and preferred pronouns.

- Using **gender neutral terms** about partners, lovers, dates, etc. is important for LGBTQ+ youth, too, because it moves away from the binary and opens the spectrum of relationships. This is a matter of sexual orientation and gender identity. It facilitates inclusion and affirmation of gay and bi youth who may not relate to heteronormative.

- **Non-binary or gender expansive** are terms that describe trans and gender expansive youth identities and experiences. The culture may not easily move along non-binary lines, but millennials instinctively understand this. By moving towards their ideas of gender and sexual identity, the culture can become a friendlier place, reducing the level of suffering experienced by LGBT+ youth.

REFLECT

- Even though the culture and language aren't changing that quickly, the way you approach LGBTQ+ youth can change everything for them!

- Try to cultivate mindfulness around your language choices. This includes being sensitive to gender and sexuality in the words you choose.

- By choosing gender neutral terms and being open to learning new things about people, you can create a warmer climate for LGBTQ+ youth.

6. THE SCHOOL-TO-PRISON PIPELINE

LEARN

The school-to-prison pipeline is a national phenomenon of pushing students out of public schools and into the juvenile and criminal justice systems. The American Civil Liberties Union (ACLU) identified students in the pipeline as poor, abused, or neglected, with learning disabilities, and desperately in need of educational support and counseling[1]. Instead, they find themselves isolated and punished in juvenile halls and prisons. "Zero-tolerance" policies criminalize small rule violations such as truancy, aggression, and drug possession.

School police officers direct students to courtrooms for discipline, whereas the same behavior in higher income communities invites treatment and understanding. Students of color are especially vulnerable to entering the school-to-prison pipeline and the discriminatory application of discipline. Snapp et al. (2015) identified LGBTQ+ youth as part of "the other marginalized youth" referred to in the "pipeline population." Without explicitly naming LGBTQ+ youth as at-risk for entering the school-to-prison pipeline, they wind up being excluded from protections and humane treatment.

The school-to-prison pipeline is a very dangerous form of discipline and legalized discrimination occurring in schools, to which LGBTQ+ youth are even more vulnerable. When their identity intersects with social, cultural and biological markers (i.e., race, religion, ethnicity, etc.) they become even more vulnerable to entering the pipeline; the risks rise exponentially. For example, African American and Latino males are at very high risk for entering the pipeline. When they are also LGBTQ+, the risk rises further and very sharply.

The school-to-prison pipeline is the most severe form of Educational Trauma. LGBTQ+ youth experience the most hostility on school campuses, and when school police are present, the danger posed to them is very high.

PRACTICE

- Are there school police officers on campus at the schools you work at or at the schools LGBTQ+ youth you care for go to?

- Take notice of the stories and schools where the police are present.

- Notice the stories where LGBTQ+ youth are also African American/Latino, poor, and/or disabled and how discipline is applied to them.

- See if there are any LGBTQ+ students you know of who are going to jail, juvenile hall, or probation for infractions you see other students receiving treatment for.

- Please consider the difference between counseling, mental health treatment, residential care—and a criminal record. Then notice that these are two very different outcomes for the same, common problems occurring in schools all over the US.

---

[1] https://www.aclu.org/issues/juvenile-justice/school-prison-pipeline

REFLECT

- If this is the first you're learning about the school-to-prison pipeline, please explore the topic further.

- Michelle Alexander (2012) in *The New Jim Crow: Mass Incarceration in the Age of Colorblindness*, detailed how segregation is alive and thriving in modern America. Segregation thrives on being initiated in schools and preserved in the prison industrial complex. This is a vast and far reaching civil rights violation.

- When caring for LGBTQ+ youth, it's imperative that we remain vigilant about the risks posed when law enforcement gets involved in their lives.

- As clinicians and educators responsible for the well-being of LGBTQ+ youth, there is an ethical responsibility to advocate for them (Abreu et al., 2016). The risks of Educational Trauma and of entering the school-to-prison pipeline, for LGBTQ+ youth, are severe and serious.

7. ECOLOGICAL SYSTEMS WORKSHEET

LEARN

At the beginning of Part II, Bronfenbrenner's ecological systems theory was explored in detail. Now that we've deepened our understanding of LGBTQ+ youth experiences at the individual (both professional and for LGBTQ+ youth), family, and community levels, it's time to explore areas of impact. This worksheet is a shortened version of the one at the beginning of Part II. It helps clinicians and educators isolate the areas within Bronfenbrenner's schema that require attention because of their negative impact on LGBTQ+ youth.

PRACTICE

Microsystems:

1. Check all of the following that currently negatively impact you or the LGBTQ+ youth you care for:

    ☐ Home

    ☐ Siblings

    ☐ Parents

    ☐ School

    ☐ Peers

    ☐ Teachers

    ☐ Neighborhood peers

    ☐ Neighbors

    ☐ Religious leaders

    ☐ Peers from religious setting

Mesosystems:

2. Check all of the following that currently negatively impact you or the LGBTQ+ youth you care for:

    ☐ Religious setting

    ☐ Home

    ☐ School

    ☐ Neighborhood

Exosystems:

3. Check all of the following that currently negatively impact you or the LGBTQ+ youth you care for:

    ☐ School board

    ☐ Local government

    ☐ Mass media

    ☐ Parents' workplace(s)

    ☐ Local businesses, charities, and community services

Macrosystems:

4. Check all of the following that currently negatively impact you or the LGBTQ+ youth you care for:

    ☐ Beliefs

    ☐ Customs

    ☐ Ideologies

    ☐ Socioeconomic status

Chronosystems:

5. Check all of the following that currently negatively impact you or the LGBTQ+ youth you care for:

    ☐ Life transitions

    ☐ Environmental events

    ☐ Socio-historical influences

REFLECT

- LGBTQ+ youth need adult caregivers to advocate for them. One way for you to do so in a way that works for you is by assessing the areas of greatest need in the practice.

- When you write down the different areas of need, you can begin prioritizing your plan of action.

- See if you can devote yourself to one area and investigate ways you can effect even minor change.

APPENDIX A
LGBTQ+ Youth Resource List

A Queer Endeavor www.aqueerendeavor.org

Trevor Project http://www.thetrevorproject.org/

World Professional Association for Transgender Health www.wpath.org

TransKids Purple Rainbow Foundation http://www.transkidspurplerainbow.org/

Human Rights Campaign www.hrc.org

Local LGBTQ+ center

PFLAG: formerly Parents, Friends, family of Lesbians and Gays—now inclusive of bisexual and transgender people, too www.pflag.org

Gender Spectrum www.genderspectrum.org

Gay and Lesbian Alliance Against Defamation www.glaad.org

Lambda Legal Aid www.lambdalegal.org

Harry Benjamin International Gender Dysphoria Association www.HBIGDA.org

Standards of Care for Gender Identity Disorders (Fifth Version) http://www.tc.umn.edu/~colem001/hbigda/hstndrd.htm

Gay Lesbian and Straight Education Network (GLSEN) https://www.glsen.org/

APPENDIX B
Parent Education and Collaboration Handout Pages

LGBTQ+ FACTS

Ryan et al. (2009) demonstrated that high family rejection is associated with LGB, and some T, youth being:

- 8.4x more likely to have attempted suicide
- 5.9x more likely to report high levels of depression
- 3.4x more likely to use illegal drugs
- 3.4x more likely to be at high risk for HIV and STDs

Moreover, Latino males retrospectively reported experiencing the highest levels of rejection for their sexual orientation during the teen years.

LGBTQ+ YOUTH AND HOMELESSNESS

- LGBTQ+ youth are disproportionately homeless compared to cisgender and straight youth.
- 40 percent of all homeless teenagers identify as LGBTQ+ (Newton, 2014).
- Homeless LGBTQ+ youth are at greater risk of:
  - *Substance abuse:* more alcohol and drug use than non-LGBTQ+ peers.
  - *High-risk sexual behavior:* selling sex for survival; exchanging sex for shelter, drugs, affection, group inclusion, and protection.
  - *Trauma:* homeless gay youth experience more physical assault and sexual abuse than homeless lesbian and bisexual youth. Transfemales experience even more violence, and both transmales and transfemales experience significant hardship locating shelters that will admit them. Gender plays a significant role in accessing homeless services, which contributes to even more harm against transyouth.
  - *Interaction with juvenile criminal justice:* family rejection and homelessness facilitate entry into the school-to-prison pipeline (Snapp et al., 2015).
  - *Mental health issues*: greater anxiety, depression, withdrawal, psychosomatic illness, and social problems.

GLSEN NATIONAL SCHOOL CLIMATE SURVEY

- 57.6% of LGBTQ+ students felt unsafe at school because of their sexual orientation.

- 43.3% of LGBTQ+ students felt unsafe at school because of their gender expression.

- 31.8% of LGBTQ+ students missed at least one day of school because they felt unsafe/uncomfortable at school.

- 10% missed more than 4 or more days of school.

- Over 1/3rd of LGBTQ+ students avoided gender segregated spaces because they felt unsafe or uncomfortable (39.4% avoided bathrooms; 37.9% avoided locker rooms).

- 85.2% of LGBTQ+ students experienced verbal assault.

- 27% of LGBTQ+ students were physically harassed.

- 13% of LGBTQ+ students were physically assaulted.

- 48.6% of LGBTQ+ students were cyberbullied.

- 71.5% of LGBTQ+ students avoided school functions.

- 65.7% of LGBTQ+ students avoided extra-curricular activities.

*Both because they felt uncomfortable or unsafe.

- 57.6% of LGBTQ+ students who were harassed or assaulted at school did not report to staff because they doubted effective interventions would occur, or that the situation might improve as a result of reporting.

- 63.5% of LGBTQ+ students who reported said staff did nothing or told the student to ignore it.

- 56.2% of LGBTQ+ students heard teachers or other staff make homophobic remarks.

- 63.5% of LGBTQ+ students heard teachers or other staff make negative remarks about gender expression.

- 66.2% of LGBTQ+ students personally experienced discriminatory practices and/or policies at school.

- 29.8% of LGBTQ+ students were disciplined for public displays of affection that were not disciplined among non-LGBTQ+ students.

- 16.7% of LGBTQ+ students reported being prevented from discussing or writing about LGBTQ+ topics.

- 14.1% of LGBTQ+ students were restricted from forming or promoting a Gay Straight Alliance.

The effects of victimization on students because of their sexual orientation or gender expression include:

- Higher levels of truancy.
- GPAs about 2 points lower than peers who were not harassed.
- Twice as likely to report lack of intention to go to college.
- Lower self-esteem.
- Higher levels of depression.
- 42.5% reported consideration of dropping out of high school because of the harassment faced at school.

INTERSECTIONALITY

- Asian/South Asian/Pacific Islander LGBTQ+ students experienced the lowest levels of victimization based on sexual orientation and gender expression.
- White LGBTQ+ students experienced the lowest levels of discrimination compared to all other races and ethnicities.

MIDDLE SCHOOL LGBTQ+ STUDENTS

- Hear more negative remarks about gender expression & sexuality.
- Report more victimization as a result of sexual orientation or gender expression.
- Are less likely to have access to LGBTQ+ curricula, GSAs, and comprehensive anti-bullying/harassment policies.

TRANS STATISTICS

- 0.3% of the adult US population is trans.
- Studies have shown that identical twins are more often both transgender than fraternal twins, indicating that there is indeed a genetic influence (Diamond, 2013.)
- Early coming out leads to more time in life as their authentic self, and can reduce negative symptoms and the need for future surgeries.
- Coming out in families with low acceptance leads to high risk of violence, rejection, and homelessness.
- Family support is associated with:
  - Lower rates of homelessness
  - Lower use of alcohol and drugs

- Lower smoking rates
- Lower rates of incarceration
- Less sex work
- Lower risk of suicidal ideation and attempt

(Transgender Discrimination Survey, Grant et al., 2011),

GROUNDING AND CENTERING MEDITATION FOR IDENTITY DEVELOPMENT

Find a comfortable position, seated, standing, or even lying down.

Notice your body and where it makes contact with the ground and/or the furniture.

Close your eyes, if you feel comfortable.

Take three deep breaths all the way down into your belly.

Feel the air inflating your chest as it enters your body through your nose.

Notice the sensations in your belly as you breathe deeply.

Now imagine there is a connector at the base of your tailbone.

Examine the width and color of this connector, then attach a cord to it.

The cord can be any color, width or thickness; there is no right or wrong here.

See the cord drop down through the floor beneath you, magically and instantly penetrating the crust of the Earth and connecting to the core.

When your grounding cord is connected to the Earth's core, you are "grounded." People often report feeling centered, energized, and radically alive.

Now that you are grounded, notice a yellow sun hovering around your forehead where it meets the bridge of your nose.

Invite this special yellow sun to collect all of your energy that may have been scattered about as you made your way through the day. Silently say to yourself:

"Yellow sun of mine, please collect any and all of my energy that may have been scattered about. Please purify it, recharge it, and return it to me."

When you are ready, allow your cleansed energy to shower down upon you like a raindrop of yellow light.

See the yellow light envelope you, and fill the space around you within the drop.

Enjoy this special space, and when you are ready, take a deep breath, and open your eyes.

APPENDIX C
Loving Kindness Practice (*Metta*)

LEARN

Loving kindness practice, also called *Metta* in Pali, is a main part of cultivating compassion and self-compassion. When practiced daily, loving kindness has transformative and healing power.

PRACTICE

Lie down, sit lotus/crisscross, or walk silently, and practice sending the following friendly wishes by silently saying to **yourself**:

- May I be healthy
- May I be happy
- May I be safe
- May I be peaceful
- May I be prosperous
- May I live easily

*Repeat many times.

Next, think of a **benefactor or mentor** (teacher or parent, aunt/uncle, etc.) and bring them fully to mind. Silently repeat:

- May you be healthy
- May you be happy
- May you be safe
- May you be peaceful
- May you be prosperous
- May you live easily

*Repeat many times.

Think of a **loved one**, bring them fully to mind and repeat the same friendly wishes as above.

Continue the practice with the following people:

- A neutral person
- A person with whom you have difficulty

Conclude with sending friendly wishes to:
- All beings everywhere

If you only have a little time, spend more time sending friendly wishes to fewer people, rather than sending fewer friendly wishes to more people.

REFLECT

- It can be challenging to send friendly wishes to people with whom one is in conflict. This is a very important time to try, because it softens you and eases your suffering.

- Some people find it easier to practice loving kindness for others than for themselves. Starting the practice by sending friendly wishes to yourself overcomes this difficulty and increases self-worth.

APPENDIX D
Substance Use Self-Test

When thinking about your drug and alcohol use, do you think it's a problem? It's ok not to write the answer; just think it through carefully.

_____
_____
_____
_____

Do you ever use drugs and/or alcohol alone? In which situations are you most likely to use drugs and/or alcohol alone?

_____
_____
_____
_____

Sometimes people use drugs and alcohol to mask pain and help them cope with life. Could this be the case for you? Explain.

_____
_____
_____
_____

In other instances, people use drugs and alcohol for mind expanding and experimental purposes. Boredom and curiosity can cause interest in drugs and alcohol. Do either of these relate to you at all? If so, how?

_____
_____
_____
_____

If anyone else saw how often you use, what would they think?

_____
_____
_____
_____

Do you only experiment with drugs and alcohol at parties? If so, would you consider partying a problem for you?

_____
_____
_____
_____

When thinking about your drug and alcohol abuse, please consider the extent to which it is helping you deal or cope with life, or if it's just a fun experiment. Explore this topic and get very clear about why you use drugs and alcohol.

_____
_____
_____
_____

APPENDIX E
Talking about Gender

Answering questions from concerned people:

1. A boy will always be a boy and a girl will always be a girl. Why should we indulge this behavior when biology is biology?

Possible answers:

    a. Well, I see where you're coming from. Our culture assigns one of two genders at birth: male or female. These assigned genders sometimes correspond with a person's genetics – sometimes not. When a person's gender identity is congruent with the one they were assigned at birth (usually base on genitals,) they are called: Cisgender. When a person's assigned gender at birth is not aligned with their internal gender identity, they are called: Transgender. Essentially, for some people their biology and internal gender identity are not aligned and the consequences are very dire. Many transgender people attempt and succeed at suicide because of the way our culture binds people to gender before they can assert it themselves. It results in very intense depression with high risks of self-harm and substance abuse.

    b. It's benevolent, compassionate, and empathic to accept students as they present themselves and wish to be seen. In our effort to make this a safe, affirming, and welcoming place for all students, we are open to biology, gender identity, and many forms of self-expression.

    c. Sometimes people are misunderstood. For trans students and gender-expansive students, the need for acceptance and belonging are just as high as for other students, and yet the rejection is even higher. Here, we wish to support the healthy development of our diverse student body with evidence-based strategies. Supporting trans and gender-expansive students reduces their risk of suicide, self-harm, sex work, substance abuse, school dropout, and underachievement.

2. How come the whole school has to make changes for one student?

Possible answers:

    a. It's often very beneficial to a whole community of people when everyone feels included and safe to be themselves. For example, sometimes people learn about themselves or others just from becoming more informed. Are there any questions you have about gender?

    b. It can be uncomfortable to learn that things we thought were very clear are actually far more nuanced and complex. I'm here for you while we all learn to be good allies and friends.

c. Empathy is one way to create bridges where conflict and separation may exist. It's ok if you don't understand, and even if you have questions; just be curious and open. It's a good way to be in the world – with everyone.

3. Are there any risks to the other students in school because of the transgender or gender-expansive students?

Possible answers:

a. The greatest risks posed here are to the trans and gender expansive students. When they feel rejected and threatened and/or harmed, the consequences can be dire. Bullying doesn't even begin to cover the problems LGBTQ+ students face in school, with the result being even higher rates of suicidal ideation, attempt, and completion than non-LGBTQ+ youth.

b. The fears around trans/gender-expansive students are often born out of ignorance, not fact. The fact is that LGBTQ+ youth suffer the most violence of all students in schools. When the schools make any changes for these students, it creates safety for everyone.

4. When the school discusses and supports transgender and gender-expansive students, doesn't it lead others to experiment too?

Possible answers:

a. Discussing the spectrum of gender and inviting creative forms of gender expression doesn't change anyone, though it may make those already thinking about it feel more comfortable expressing themselves. Other people can't influence young people to become LGBTQ+; however, they can influence their sense of self. The rejection LGBTQ+ youth face decreases their sense of worthiness and hope for future love/success. In other words, not talking about it can have negative effects. Talking about it can lead LGBTQ+ youth to feel more comfortable being open about themselves.

5. Is it just phase? Could all this talk and school accommodation cause more students to "experiment" with their gender or claim "trans"?

Possible answers:

a. When students come out as trans, a lot has led up to that point. They've likely received some support and education to realize they are trans and to be willing to come out. It's unlikely that students unaffected by the gender binary will suddenly find themselves experimenting with being trans.

b. The link between one person coming out and another doing so as well is unsupported unless that person was already on the same trajectory. There are many more nuances in gender expression than the binary of male and female. When one person expresses themselves outside the binary, it frees up others to be their authentic selves, too.

6. Will male students start coming to school and saying they're trans just so they can change in the girls' locker room?

Possible answers:

a. The risks of coming out as trans are really high for some people. It's very unusual for people to use gender as a predatory technique. That we associate gender with predation like this is a mistake. There is evidence that predators use grooming behaviors to lure victims and preserve their trust, as well as their parents' trust. The profiles of a student who is a predator and a person with gender dysphoria are very different. We don't have evidence to support your concern; however, I appreciate you sharing it with me so I could share what I know, too.

b. There are a number of ways school staff work together to support students. For some students, the suffering they face in being assigned one gender at birth when internally they know themselves to be something else is beyond bearable. It exceeds the kind of depression we commonly see in teens, as well as in people with severe depressive disorders. When school staff work together to support the needs of trans/gender-expansive students, they are offering equitable education.

APPENDIX F
Talking about Gender

– Confidential –
Gender Support Plan

The purpose of this document is to create shared understandings about the ways in which the student's authentic gender will be accounted for and supported at school. School staff, caregivers and the student should work together to complete this document. Ideally, each will spend time completing the various sections to the best of their ability and then come together to review sections and confirm shared agreements about using the plan. Please note that there is a separate document to plan for a student formally communicating information about a change in their gender status at school.

School/District _____ Today's Date _____
Name Student Uses: _____ Name on Birth Certificate: _____
Student's Gender Identity _____ Assigned Sex at Birth _____ Student Grade Level _____
Date of Birth _____ Sibling(s)/Grade(s) _____ / _____ _____ / _____
Parent(s), Guardian(s), or Caregiver(s) /relation to student
_____ / _____   _____ / _____
_____ / _____   _____ / _____
Meeting participants: _____

PARENT/GUARDIAN INVOLVEMENT

Are guardian(s) of this student aware and supportive of their child's gender status?   ____Yes   ____No

If not, what considerations must be accounted for in implementing this plan? _____
_____
_____

CONFIDENTIALITY, PRIVACY AND DISCLOSURE

How public or private will information about this student's gender be (check all that apply)?

- ____ District staff will be aware (Superintendent, Student Support Services, District Psychologist, etc.)
  Specify the adult staff members:

- ____ Site level leadership/administration will know (Principal, head of school, counselor, etc.)
  Specify the adult staff members:

- ____ Teachers and/or other school staff will know
  Specify the adult staff members:

- ____ Student will not be openly "out," but some students are aware of the student's gender
  Specify the students:

- ____ Student is open with others (adults and peers) about gender

- ____ Other – describe: _____

If the student has asserted a degree of privacy, what steps will be taken if that privacy is compromised, or is believed to have been compromised? _____
_____
_____

www.genderspectrum.org • 510-788-4412 • info@genderspectrum.org

Rev. 090517

Used with permission of Gender Spectrum (www.genderspectrum.org)

How will a teacher/staff member respond to any questions about the student's gender from:

Other students? _____

_____

Staff members? _____

_____

Parents/community? _____

_____

STUDENT SAFETY

Who will be the student's "go to adult" on campus? _____

If this person is not available, what should student do? _____

What, if any, will be the process for periodically checking in with the student and/or family? ____

_____

What are expectations in the event the student is feeling unsafe and how will student signal their need for help:

During class _____

On the yard _____

In the halls _____

Other _____

Other safety concerns/questions: _____

_____

_____

What should the student's parents do if they are concerned about how others are treating their child at school?

_____

NAMES, PRONOUNS AND STUDENT RECORDS

What name and gender marker are listed on the student's identity documents? _____

Name/gender marker entered into the Student Information System _____

Name to be used when referring to the student _____ Pronouns _____

Can the student's name/gender marker be reflected in the SIS? _____ If so, how? If not, why not?

_____

_____

If not, what adjustments can be made to protect this student's privacy (see below)? _____

_____

_____

Who will be the point person at school for ensuring these adjustments are made and communicated as needed?

_____

How will instances be handled in which the incorrect name or pronoun are used by staff members? _____

_____

By students? _____

Used with permission of Gender Spectrum (www.genderspectrum.org)

If unable to change the student's profile in the student information system, how will the student's privacy be accounted for and maintained in the following situations or contexts:

- During registration_____
- Completing enrollment_____
- With substitute teachers_____
- Standardized tests_____
- School photos_____
- IEPs/Other Services_____
- Student cumulative file_____
- After-school programs_____
- Lunch lines_____
- Taking attendance_____
- Teacher grade book(s)_____
- Official school-home communication_____
- Unofficial school-home communication (PTA/other)_____
- Outside district personnel or providers_____
- Summons to office_____
- Yearbook_____
- Student ID/library cards_____
- Posted lists_____
- Distribution of texts or other school supplies_____
- Assignment of IT accounts/email address_____
- PA announcements_____

If the student's guardians are not aware and/or supportive of the student's gender status, how will school-home communications be handled?

_____
_____

What are some other ways the school needs to anticipate the student's privacy being compromised? How will these be handled?

_____
_____

USE OF FACILITIES

Student will use the following bathroom(s) on campus_____

Student will change clothes in the following place(s)_____

If student/parent have questions/concerns about facilities, who should they contact?_____

What are the expectations regarding the use of facilities for any class trips?_____

_____

What are the expectations regarding rooming for any overnight trips?_____

_____

Are there any questions or concerns about the student's access to facilities?_____

Used with permission of Gender Spectrum (www.genderspectrum.org)

EXTRA CURRICULAR ACTIVITIES

In what extra-curricular programs or activities will the student be participating (sports, theater, clubs, etc)?
_____
_____

What steps will be necessary for supporting the student there?_____
_____
_____

Does the student participate in an after-school program?_____

What steps will be necessary for supporting the student there?_____
_____
_____

Questions/Notes: _____
_____

OTHER CONSIDERATIONS

Does the student have any sibling(s) at school?_____ Factors to be considered regarding sibling's needs?
_____
_____
_____

Does the school have a dress code? _____ How will this be handled?_____
_____
_____

Are there lessons, units, content or other activities coming up this year to consider (growth and development, swim unit, social justice units, name projects, dance instruction, Pride events, school dances etc.)?_____
_____
_____

Are there any specific social dynamics with other students, families or staff members that need to be discussed or accounted for?_____
_____
_____
_____

What training(s) will the school engage in to build capacity for working with gender-expansive students? How will the school work to create more gender inclusive conditions for all students?_____
_____
_____
_____

Does the student use school- or district-provided transportation services? If so, how will the student's gender be accounted for?_____
_____
_____

Used with permission of Gender Spectrum (www.genderspectrum.org)

Are there any other questions, concerns or issues to discuss? _____

_____
_____
_____
_____
_____
_____
_____

SUPPORT PLAN REVIEW AND REVISION

How will this plan be monitored over time? _____

_____

What will be the process should the student, family, or school wish to revisit any aspects of the plan (or seek additions to the plan)? _____

_____

What are specific follow-ups or action items emerging from this meeting and who is responsible for them?

Action Item	Who?	When?

Date/Time of next meeting or check-in _____ Location _____

Used with permission of Gender Spectrum (www.genderspectrum.org)

– Confidential –
Gender Communication Plan

This document supports the necessary planning for a student to communicate with the school community a change in one or more aspects of their gender from its commonly assumed status to something else. Its purpose is to create the most favorable conditions for a successful experience, and to identify the specific actions that will be taken by the student, school, family, or other support providers.

School/District _____ Today's Date _____
Student's Preferred Name _____ Legal Name _____
Student's Gender _____ Assigned Sex at Birth _____ Student Grade Level _____
Date of Birth _____ Sibling(s)/Grade(s) _____ / _____ _____ / _____
Parent(s)/Guardian(s)/Caregiver(s) /relation to student
_____ / _____   _____ / _____
_____ / _____   _____ / _____

What does the student wish to communicate about their gender (change in identity, expression, etc.)?
_____

How urgent is the student's need? Is the child currently experiencing <u>distress</u> regarding their gender?
_____

PARENT/GUARDIAN INVOLVEMENT

Are guardian(s) of this student aware and supportive of their child's gender communication? ____Yes ____No
If not, what considerations must be accounted for in implementing this plan? _____
_____
_____

INITIAL PLANNING MEETING

When will the initial planning meeting take place? _____ Where will it occur? _____
Who will be the members of the team supporting the student's communication?

- ❑ Student   _____
- ❑ Parent(s)   _____ _____ _____
- ❑ School Staff   _____ _____ _____
                   _____ _____ _____
- ❑ Other   _____ _____ _____

COMMUNICATION DETAILS: WHAT IS THE STUDENT'S IDEAL SCENARIO?

What is the specific information that the student wishes to convey? (be specific)? _____
_____
_____

What requests are being made of others (new name, pronouns, use of facilities, etc.)? _____

www.genderspectrum.org • 510-788-4412 • info@genderspectrum.org

Rev. 090517

Used with permission of Gender Spectrum (www.genderspectrum.org)

Imagine that this process goes **exactly** as the student wishes. What does it look/sound like? Describe how this information will be shared (i.e. a lesson about gender combined with announcement from teacher(s); an assembly where student will share information; a written communication; etc.). Be as specific as possible about what occurs.

_____
_____
_____
_____
_____

With whom and when will this information be shared?
- ❑ With peers in the student's class only   Date: _____
- ❑ With peers in the student's grade level   Date: _____
- ❑ With some/all students at school (specify)_____ Date: _____
- ❑ Other (specify) _____

Who will lead the lessons/activities framing the student's announcement?_____

What will the lesson/activities be? _____
_____
_____

Will the student be present for the lesson/sharing of info about their gender? _____

If yes, what role, if any, does the student want to play in the process?_____
_____

Will the parent(s)/caregiver(s) be present for the lesson/sharing of info? _____

If yes, what role, if any, will they play in the process?_____
_____

Once the information is shared, what parameters/expectations will be set regarding approaching the student?
_____
_____

Other notes, considerations or questions _____
_____

KEY DECISIONS PRIOR TO STUDENT'S COMMUNICATION

Communications with Other Families

Will any sort of information be shared with other families about the student's gender? _____

With whom: ____ Families in child's grade   ____ Whole School   ____Other (specify)_____

Who will be responsible for creating this? _____ When will it be sent? _____

How will it be distributed? _____

*What specific information will be shared? _____
_____
_____

Questions/Notes: _____
_____

Used with permission of Gender Spectrum (www.genderspectrum.org)

* see sample letters

Training for School Staff

Will there be specific training about this student's gender with school staff?_____ When? _____

Who will be conducting the training? _____ What will be the content of the training?

_____

_____

Questions/Notes: _____

_____

_____

Parent Information Night/ Class Meeting with Parents About Gender Diversity

Will there be specific training for school community members?_____ When? _____

Who'll conduct it? _____ Will it reference the student's gender? _____

What will be the content of the training? _____

_____

_____

Questions/Notes: _____

_____

Identifying and Enlisting Parent Allies

Are there any parents/adults in the community you would like to enlist in support of the child's communication?
If so, who?_____

When will you speak with them?_____ What will be your request? _____

_____

Questions/Notes: _____

_____

Identifying and Enlisting Peer Allies

Are there other students you would like to enlist in support of the child's communication?_____
If so, who?_____

When will they be spoken with?_____ What requests will be made? _____

_____

_____

Questions/Notes: _____

Siblings

Does the student have any siblings at the school?_____ What needs to be considered for them?

Training in their classroom(s)? _____ Emotional Support? _____

_____

_____

Questions/Notes: _____

_____

_____

Used with permission of Gender Spectrum (www.genderspectrum.org)

POSSIBLE ACTIONS AFTER COMMUNICATION TAKES PLACE

Does the student currently have a Gender Support Plan? _____ If so, what needs to be modified? _____
_____

What steps will be taken following the communication to check on the student's status/well-being? _____
_____
_____

Questions/Notes: _____
_____
_____

TIMELINE

Which of the following will take place in relation to this student's gender communication, when will it occur and who will be responsible for making it happen?

Activity	Date	Lead
❑ Initial Planning Meeting	_____	_____
❑ Lessons/Activities with Other Students	_____	_____
❑ Communications with Other Families	_____	_____
❑ Training for School Staff	_____	_____
❑ Parent Information Night About Gender Diversity	_____	_____
❑ Identifying and Enlisting Parent Allies	_____	_____
❑ Identifying and Enlisting Peer Allies	_____	_____

What are the specific follow-ups or action items emerging from this meeting and who is responsible for them?

Action Item	Who?	When?

Used with permission of Gender Spectrum (www.genderspectrum.org)

References

> For your convenience, purchasers can download
> and print handouts from www.pesi.com/LGBTQYouth

Abreu, R. L., Black, W. W., Mosley, D. V., & Fedewa, A. L. (2016). LGBTQ youth bullying experiences in schools: The role of school counselors within a system of oppression. *Journal of Creativity in Mental Health, 11*(3-4), 325-342. Retrieved March 9, 2017, from http://www.tandfonline.com/doi/pdf/10.1080/15401383.2016.1214092.

Alexander, M. (2012). *The new Jim Crow: Mass incarceration in the age of colorblindness.* New York, NY: The New Press.

Alsenas, L. (2008). *Gay America: Struggle for equality.* New York, NY: Amulet Books.

American School Counselor Association. (2010). American School Counselor Association's Ethical Standards for School Counselors. *PsycEXTRA Dataset.* doi:10.1037/e504792012-001.

Black, D. L. (2009). *Milk: A pictorial history of Harvey Milk.* New York, NY: Newmarket Press.

Blanchard, R. (1989). The Concept of Autogynephilia and the Typology of Male Gender Dysphoria. *The Journal of Nervous and Mental Disease, 177*(10), 616-623. doi:10.1097/00005053-198910000-00004.

Bloom, P. (2016). *Against Empathy: The case for rational compassion.* New York, NY: Harper Collins.

Boylan, J. F. (2003). *She's not there: A life in two genders.* New York, NY: Broadway Books.

Brill, S., & Kenney, L. (2016). *The transgender teen: A handbook for parents and professionals supporting transgender and non-binary teens.* San Francisco, CA: Cleis Press.

Brill, S. A., & Pepper, R. (2008). *The transgender child.* San Francisco, CA: Cleis Press.

Bronfenbrenner, U. (1979). *Ecology of Human Development: Experiments by Nature and Design.* Cambridge, MA: Harvard University Press.

Bronski, M., Pellegrini, A., & Amico, M. (2013). *"You can tell just by looking" And 20 other myths about LGBT life and people.* Boston, MA: Beacon Press.

Browning, F. (2016). *The fate of gender: Nature, nurture, and the human future.* New York, NY: Bloomsbury, an imprint of Bloomsbury Publishing Plc.

Cass, V. C. (1979). Homosexuality Identity Formation. *Journal of Homosexuality, 4*(3), 219-235. doi:10.1300/j082v04n03_01.

Coolhart, D., Baker, A., Farmer, S., Malaney, M., & Shipman, D. (2012). Therapy with Transsexual Youth and Their Families: A Clinical Tool for Assessing Youths Readiness for Gender Transition. *Journal of Marital and Family Therapy, 39*(2), 223-243. doi:10.1111/j.1752-0606.2011.00283.x.

Crenshaw, K. (2010). *Critical race theory: The key writings; that formed the movement.* New York, NY: New Press.

Dabrowski, K. (1964). *Positive Disintegration.* Boston, MA: Little Brown.

Dawson, J. (2015). *This book is gay.* Naperville, IL: Sourcebooks.

Dhejne, C., Oberg, K., Arver, S., & Landen, M. (2014). An Analysis of All Applications for Sex Reassignment Surgery in Sweden, 1960-2010: Prevalence, Incidence, and Regrets. *Archives of Sexual Behavior, 43*(8), 1535-1545. doi:10.1007/s10508-014-0300-8.

Diamond, M. (2013). Transsexuality Among Twins: Identity Concordance, Transition, Rearing, and Orientation. *International Journal of Transgenderism, 14*(1), 24-38. doi:10.1080/15532739.2013.750222.

Dreger, A. D. (2016). *Galileo's middle finger: Heretics, activists, and one scholar's search for justice.* New York, NY: Penguin Books.

Edwards, K. M., & Sylaska, K. M. (2012). The Perpetration of Intimate Partner Violence among LGBTQ College Youth: The Role of Minority Stress. *Journal of Youth and Adolescence, 42*(11), 1721-1731. doi:10.1007/s10964-012-9880-6.

Ehrensaft, D. (2011). *Gender born, gender made: Raising healthy gender-nonconforming children.* New York, NY: Experiment.

Espelage, D., Merrin, G., & Hatchel, T. (2016). Peer Victimization and Dating Violence Among LGBTQ Youth: The Impact of School Violence and Crime on Mental Health Outcomes. *Youth Violence and Juvenile Justice.* Retrieved March 8, 2017, from https://doi.org/10.1177/1541204016680408.

Falender, C. A., & Shafranske, E. P. (2013). *Clinical supervision: A competency-based approach.* Washington, DC: American Psychological Association.

Fausto-Sterling, A. (2000). *Sexing the body: Gender politics and the construction of sexuality.* New York, NY: Basic Books.

Fernandez, R., Esteva, I., Gomez-Gil, E., Rumbo, T., Almaraz, M. C., Roda, E., Haro-Mora, J.J., Guillamon, A, Pasaro, E. (2014). The (CA)n Polymorphism of ERB Gene is Associated with FtM Transsexualism. *The Journal of Sexual Medicine, 11*(3), 720-728. doi:10.1111/jsm.12398.

Fish, L. S., & Harvey, R. G. (2005). *Nurturing queer youth: Family therapy transformed.* New York, NY: Norton.

Gilbert, P. (2009). *The compassionate mind: A new approach to life's challenges.* Oakland, CA: New Harbinger.

Gray, L. (2015, November 23). The Spectrum of Educational Trauma. Retrieved from http://www.huffingtonpost.com/leeanne-gray-psyd/the-spectrum-of-education_b_8619536.html.

Gray, L. J. (2016). *Self-compassion for teens: 129 activities & practices to cultivate kindness*. Eau Claire, WI: Pesi Pub & Media.

Hayes, S. C., Strosahl, K. D., & Wilson, K. G. (2016). *Acceptance and commitment therapy: The process and practice of mindful change*. New York, NY: Guilford Press.

Health Research Funding. (2014, November 26). 15 Notable Ambiguous Genitalia Statistics. Retrieved June 21, 2017, from http://healthresearchfunding.org/15-notable-ambiguous-genitalia-statistics/.

Jennings, J. (2016). *Being Jazz: My life as a (transgender teen)*. New York, NY: Crown.

Johansson, A., Sundbom, E., Hojerback, T., & Bodlund, O. (2009). A Five-Year Follow-Up Study of Swedish Adults with Gender Identity Disorder. *Archives of Sexual Behavior, 39*(6), 1429-1437. doi:10.1007/s10508-009-9551-1.

Kinsey, A. C., Pomeroy, W. B., & Martin, C. E. (1998). *Sexual behavior in the human male* (Reprint ed.). Bloomington, IN: Indiana University Press.

Klein, F. (1993). *The Bisexual Option: Second Edition*. NJ: American Institute of Bisexuality.

Kosciw, J. G., Greytak, E. A., Giga, N. M., Villenas, C., & Danischewski, D. J. (n.d.). *The 2015 National School Climate Survey*. Retrieved January 1, 2017, from https://www.glsen.org/sites/default/files/GLSEN%202015%20National%20School%20Climate%20Survey%20%28NSCS%29%20-%20Executive%20Summary_0.pdf.

Lev, A. I. (2004). *Transgender emergence: Therapeutic guidelines for working with gender-variant people and their families*. New York, NY: The Haworth Clinical Practice Press.

Levine, S. B., Brown, G., Coleman, E., Cohen-Kettenis, P., Hage, J., Van Maasdam, J., … Schaeffer, L. C. (1998, June 15). Standards of Care. Retrieved December 18, 2016, from http://www.tc.umn.edu/~colem001/hbigda/hstndrd.htm.

Losen, D. J., & Gillespie, J. (2012, August 07). Opportunities suspended: The disparate impact of disciplinary exclusion from school (Rep.). Retrieved September 4, 2017, from http://civilrightsproject.ucla.edu/resources/projects/center-for-civil-rights-remedies/school-to-prison-folder/federal-reports/upcoming-ccrr-research.

Luders, E., Sánchez, F. J., Gaser, C., Toga, A. W., Narr, K. L., Hamilton, L. S., & Vilain, E. (2009). Regional gray matter variation in male-to-female transsexualism. *NeuroImage, 46*(4), 904-907. doi:10.1016/j.neuroimage.2009.03.048.

Marshal, M. P., Friedman, M. S., Stall, R., King, K. M., Miles, J., Gold, M. A., . . . Morse, J. Q. (2008). Sexual orientation and adolescent substance use: A meta-analysis and methodological review. *Addiction, 103*(4), 546-556. doi:10.1111/j.1360-0443.2008.02149.x.

McCormick, M. (2016). *Bullying Experiences and Resilience in LGBTQ Youth* (Doctoral dissertation, Western Michigan University, 2016). Kalamazoo, MI: Western Michigan University Libraries. doi:http://scholarworks.wmich.edu/dissertations/2473/.

Newton, D. E. (2014). *LGBT youth issues today: A reference handbook*. Santa Barbara, CA: ABC-CLIO.

Orr, A., & Baum, J. (2015). Schools in Transition: A Guide to Supporting Transgender Students in K-12 Schools. Retrieved August 24, 2017, from https://www.genderspectrum.org/staging/wp-content/uploads/2015/08/Schools-in-Transition-2015.pdf.

Peters, G., & Wooley, J. T. (2017). Voter Turnout in Presidential Elections. Retrieved March 22, 2017, from http://www.presidency.ucsb.edu/data/turnout.php.

Poteat, V. P., Sinclair, K. O., Digiovanni, C. D., Koenig, B. W., & Russell, S. T. (2012). Gay-Straight Alliances Are Associated With Student Health: A Multischool Comparison of LGBTQ and Heterosexual Youth. *Journal of Research on Adolescence, 23*(2), 319-330. doi:10.1111/j.1532-7795.2012.00832.x.

Rametti, G., Carrillo, B., Gomez-Gil, E., Junque, C., Segovia, S., Gomez, Á., & Guillamon, A. (2011). White matter microstructure in female to male transsexuals before cross-sex hormonal treatment. A diffusion tensor imaging study. *Journal of Psychiatric Research, 45*(2), 199-204. doi:10.1016/j.jpsychires.2010.05.006.

Ryan, C., Huebner, D., Diaz, R. M., & Sanchez, J. (2009). Family Rejection as a Predictor of Negative Health Outcomes in White and Latino Lesbian, Gay, and Bisexual Young Adults. *Pediatrics, 123*(1), 346-352. doi:10.1542/peds.2007-3524.

Ryan, C., Russell, S. T., Huebner, D., Diaz, R., & Sanchez, J. (2010). Family Acceptance in Adolescence and the Health of LGBT Young Adults. *Journal of Child and Adolescent Psychiatric Nursing, 23*(4), 205-213. doi:10.1111/j.1744-6171.2010.00246.x.

Savin-Williams, R. C. (1990). *Gay and lesbian youth: Expressions of identity* (1st ed.). New York, NY: Hemisphere Publishing / Taylor & Francis.

Shepard, J., & Barrett, J. (2009). *The meaning of Matthew: My son's murder in Laramie, and a world transformed*. New York, NY: Hudson Street Press.

Siegel, D. J., & Hartzell, M. (2014). *Parenting from the inside out: How a deeper self-understanding can help you raise children who thrive* (10th anniversary ed.). New York, NY: Jeremy Tarcher/Penguin.

Siegel, D. J. (2014). *Brainstorm: The power and purpose of the teenage brain*. Brunswick, Vic.: Scribe Publications.

Snapp, S. D., Hoenig, J. M., Fields, A., & Russell, S. T. (2015). Messy, Butch, and Queer. *Journal of Adolescent Research, 30*(1), 57-82. doi:10.1177/0743558414557625.

Testa, R. J., Coolhart, D., & Peta, J. (2015). *The gender quest workbook: A guide for teens and young adults exploring gender identity*. Oakland, CA: Instant Help Books, An Imprint of New Harbinger Publications.

Thomas, P. L., Profilio, B., Carr, P., & Gorlewski, J. (2015). *Pedagogies of kindness and respect: On the lives and education of children*. New York, NY: Peter Lang.

Wallace, G. (2016, November 30). Voter turnout at 20-year low in 2016. Retrieved March 22, 2017, from http://www.cnn.com/2016/11/11/politics/popular-vote-turnout-2016/index.html.

Weyers, S., Elaut, E., Sutter, P. D., Gerris, J., T'sjoen, G., Heylens, G., . . . Verstraelen, H. (2009). Long-term Assessment of the Physical, Mental, and Sexual Health among Transsexual Women. *The Journal of Sexual Medicine, 6*(3), 752-760. doi:10.1111/j.1743-6109.2008.01082.x.

Wu, K. (2016, October 25). Between the (gender) lines: The science of transgender identity [Web log post]. Retrieved June 21, 2017, from http://sitn.hms.harvard.edu/flash/2016/gender-lines-science-transgender-identity/.

Zeigler, C. (2016). *Fair play: How LGBT athletes are claiming their rightful place in sports.* Brooklyn, NY: Edge Of Sports c/o Akashic Books.

Made in the USA
Middletown, DE
10 September 2019